Conspiracy of Silence

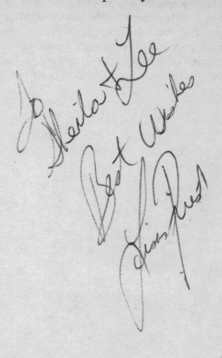

LISA PRIEST

Conspiracy of Silence

An M&S Paperback from
McClelland & Stewart Inc.
The Canadian Publishers

An M&S Paperback from McClelland & Stewart Inc.

First printing February 1989

Copyright © 1989 by Lisa Priest

Canadian Cataloguing in Publication Data

Priest, Lisa
    Conspiracy of silence

ISBN 0-7710-7152-3

1. Osborne, Helen Betty, d. 1971.   2. Murder –
Manitoba – The Pas.   3. Trials (Murder) – Manitoba –
The Pas.   4. Cree Indians – Criminal justice system.
5. Indians of North America – Manitoba – Criminal
justice system.   6. Cree Indians – Government
relations.   7. Indians of North America – Canada –
Government relations – 1951–   .*   I. Title.

HV6535.C33P3 1989   364.1'523'08997071272
                              C89-093148-8

Cover design by Tad Aronowicz

Typesetting by Q Composition

Printed and bound in Canada

McClelland & Stewart Inc.
The Canadian Publishers
481 University Avenue
Toronto, Ontario
M5G 2E9

Contents

"Justice is a temporary thing that must at last come to an end; but the conscience is eternal and will never die."

—Martin Luther

"People still ask me, 'Come on, did everyone in town really know who the killers were?' and I said, 'Yeah, we all knew but we didn't say anything.' "

—A resident of The Pas

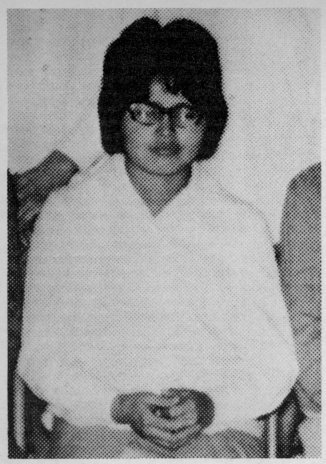

Helen Betty Osborne, 1952 – 1971 (photo: Brian E. Roque)

PART ONE

Betty

CHAPTER ONE

November 13, 1971, was cold and miserable. The sky was dark grey. Hardly anyone was out, except one very avid fisherman, fifty-one-year-old Steve Gurba. Sporting a fishing cap and warm parka, he coaxed his fourteen-year-old son, Kenny, into going fishing off the point at Clearwater Lake on that dreary Saturday morning.

Steve and Kenny sat, motionless and quiet, for a couple of hours waiting for a bite. Nothing. A little while longer and still nothing. It was plain to Kenny that his father's promised pail of trout wasn't going to materialize. Bored and curious, he took a short walk up to a gravel strip to the dense bush a couple of hundred feet southeast, looking for rabbit tracks.

As Steve watched Kenny walk towards the bush he felt a cooler, brisk wind come up. The only sounds were those of the howling wind and the spruce and pine whipping in the breeze. He noted that another fisherman, who seemed to be minding his own business, had begun fishing several hundred feet away. Just then Steve turned his head to see his son running down the gravel strip alongside the bush. He was panting.

On his hunt for rabbit tracks Kenny had spotted a nude, badly mutilated woman, clad only in thick, black rubber boots. Her killer hadn't counted on Kenny Gurba getting curious that day.

Kenny didn't scream or cry but calmly told his father,

"I found something, but it wasn't rabbits." Steve then asked his son if he was sure of his find. "I asked him twice and he said yes," Steve Gurba recalled, adding that he hadn't wanted to double-check. "And I said let's go for the Mounties." It must have been the most grotesque sight Kenny had ever seen, but he says it didn't really bother him.

Together, Kenny and his dad drove to the closest phone – up the gravel strip from the point, across the highway to The Pas Airport, a few hundred feet southwest. As they walked to the flight services desk, they noticed an RCMP officer from the air services division. Kenny described what he'd found.

The three men drove across the road down to the gravel pit to the pumphouse, located a few hundred feet from where Kenny had spotted the corpse. He and the officer walked to the murder scene but were careful not to get too close to the body. Although the officer didn't specialize in criminal police work he knew they shouldn't disturb the scene or anything that might be considered physical evidence.

A quick glance at the scene confirmed Kenny's find, and the officer made mental notes of the details. He called the local Royal Canadian Mounted Police.

As soon as the officer relayed news of the murder, the RCMP in the rural and town detachments of The Pas went into action. They called for a backup from the Dauphin detachment down south: they would need a dog man, a supervisor, a helicopter to get the aerial view of the murder scene, and a police photographer. A top team of investigators would be needed to gather every piece of evidence, every splatter of blood, hair, and thread of clothing. Of paramount concern was the possibility that a wacko was on the loose and ready to strike again. No effort could be spared.

Kenny and his dad were told to stay near the pumphouse, which was being cordoned off with ribbon, until the police took their statements. Steve Gurba made use of the time to do some fishing off the point. "I wasn't too concerned over it," Gurba recalled. "It didn't bother me, probably because I didn't see it and I didn't want anything to do with it."

*   *   *

Constable Tom Boyle, then twenty-four, was comfortably resting at his downtown home when he got a call from fellow cop Don "Giggles" Knight shortly before 1:00 P.M. There had been a murder at the pumphouse. Too hurried to change out of his ratty blue jeans and torn T-shirt, Boyle grabbed his coat, jumped into his car, and raced down to pick up Knight.

As Boyle pulled into the drive of Knight's house he thumped the steering wheel – they needed bags to gather evidence. Knight jumped in and they stopped at a convenience store, yanking packages of Ziploc bags, rolls of tape and Glad bags off the shelves and quickly paying the cashier. Back then, Knight said, officers didn't have ready-made kits for collecting evidence that they could take on the road with them. They threw the supplies in the back seat, drove north down Highway 10. At the turn onto the provincial trunk Highway 287, the road leading to the pumphouse, several RCMP cruiser cars with their familiar black and white markings were hugging the shoulder. Boyle and Knight jumped out where about a half-dozen police "preserved" the scene. It was around 1:45 P.M.

One of the most important aspects of a homicide investigation is preserving the scene. Officers seal off the area not letting anyone in or out and not disturbing anything that could be crucial to the investigation. They collect physical evidence, make careful measurements of footprints leading up to the body, and look for evidence, such as blood, clothing, or a murder weapon.

While some officers are taking measurements of a scene, others do interviews, trying to find suspects, and collect evidence. From then on, it's mostly footwork and door-to-door interviews until they can make an arrest.

Knight and Boyle met with Sergeant Larry Grosenick of Dauphin, the main organizer on the case. His job was to administrate, give out orders, supervise the officers, make sure continuity was maintained in the investigation, and keep track of the various reports. A homicide guarantees a mountain of paperwork.

Grosenick reeled off a list of jobs. Knight, twenty-four, a constable with five years' experience, was given the plum job of chief investigator and scene man; Corporal Harold Bielert would assist.

Boyle, a husky constable with four years' experience, was given the more junior and perhaps less pleasant job of looking after the body. Although Boyle knew his job was as important as any other officer's, he was disappointed. He'd become a cop to do street work, to be in the front line. Looking after the body meant he would have to sit in the morgue until it was identified, assist at the autopsy and collect fingernail scrapings, blood and any other evidence that might be considered important to the investigation. It was a gruesome and somewhat tedious job.

Other officers would have to interview people, preserve the scene, take aerial photographs and search the highway and the area for miles around for the murder weapon.

After Grosenick reeled off his orders, Knight and Bielert went over to the scene. The atmosphere, while tense, was businesslike. They walked several hundred feet east of the body and came in from behind, careful to steer completely clear of the footprints. Knight was careful to make mental notes as he approached the body; he did some of his best work from gathering his first impressions at the scene.

Wedged in the blood-stained snow was the body of a badly beaten and stabbed Native woman. She appeared to be in her teens. Her hair was splayed out and hung thickly in matted clumps. Dozens of stab wounds riddled her partially frozen body. What had been soft, brown skin was grotesquely swollen and purple, flecked with what appeared to be tiny stab wounds. Someone had snapped.

Knight stared at the mangled and bloodied victim and pulled out his notepad, carefully writing down observations as they came to him. One of the first things he noted was that someone must have stomped on her face with his boot or shoe, shortly before she was left for dead. That boot blast had caused blood to squirt from the many holes that riddled her head, creating a halo of blood two to three feet in every direction. It had also left her face a mangled, bruised piece of pulp and flattened her nose. There was a five-centimetre cut to her left ear, almost slicing it in half. As well, there were pine needles and twigs tangled in her hair.

"It appeared to me, the boots had been put to her," Knight recalled later. "There was blood all around her head. Someone kicked her in the head in her final resting spot."

This was the most brutal and vicious homicide Knight had ever seen. As a constable in The Pas, Manitoba, a rough cowboy town, he thought he'd seen it all. He'd already worked on three homicides. He'd seen a victim's brains blown out with a single shotgun blast, and another hacked to pieces with an axe. Never had he seen anything like this.

Knight edged in closer to the body. He knew the murder weapon must be something blunt. A knife, he thought, would make cleaner gashes deep in the flesh. Most of the puncture wounds in this victim were rough; the skin had folded into them. One particular wound that caught his attention was near her right eye, close to the nose. It was a deep, round gash surrounded by caked-on blood. As well, her face and abdomen were smeared with blood and the jaw area was bruised and swollen.

Three days later, an autopsy performed at Winnipeg

General Hospital by Dr. Donald Wills Penner would reveal that the murder could have only been the work of a deranged, frenzied killer.

Page 2 of the autopsy report coolly described the body: length 154 centimetres; weight 46 kilograms; age, 19; hair color, black; eyes, brown. The victim weighed 101 pounds and was 5 feet, 1 inch tall.

Dr. Penner had counted as many as fifty stab wounds to the body. Most of them were gashes to the head, chest and back area, many of them made on the left side of her body when she was naked. They were probably made with a flat-lathed screwdriver. One of the wounds to the lower back of the head was 5.5 centimetres deep, 4.5 centimetres into the brain. It was an especially difficult wound to make. The weapon would have had to smash through a centimetre of bone before it could puncture the brain matter.

Other wounds were so small they were difficult to count; some were so close to each other they had only stretched and lightly wounded the skin. Her face was cracked in half and her upper teeth could be removed like a denture plate. As well, underneath her cracked scalp were swirls of blood over her brain, and there was a large amount of blood laying dormant in the back of her throat. Her right kidney was torn and bleeding.

Tests showed that the victim had been intoxicated and had died of shock and haemorrhaging due to multiple injuries, especially to the head. It was one of the most gruesome autopsies Dr. Penner would perform in fifty years of practice. But there was no evidence of sexual intercourse. So what was the motive?

Knight noticed five sets of tracks going into the scene and five sets of tracks going out. Within that area, he noted three distinct sets of footprints. "One shoe was an Oxford style (flat heel and sole), one had a squared pattern on the heel and the other had a cross-cut in the upper left part of the heel," he recalled. Measurements taken later would reveal the prints were 11 1/2, 12, and 12 1/2 inches long, average- and larger than average-sized feet. Knight wasn't able to distinguish if the footprints had been made by shoes or boots.

Knight noticed one set of footprints on each side of the body, leading him to believe there had been two people heavily involved in the killing. Knight could tell the victim had been dragged by the arms because her black boots made a heeled impression in the snow all the way up to her final resting spot, seventy-five feet deep into the bush. The two sets of footprints branched off and separated. Two people had walked out of the murder scene as much as fifteen feet apart, heading west, leaving the bloodied victim for dead in the wilderness.

The killers initially dumped the mangled body forty-three feet deep in the bush; her body made a bloodied imprint in the snow. But the killers must have had second thoughts and decided it still wasn't hidden well enough, so they dragged her by the arms thirty-two feet east into the bush. In all, she was one hundred and forty-four feet away from the pumphouse.

The police decided not to take casts of the killers' footprints. Footprint casts are valuable if they match specific characteristics of the footwear of the accused: for example the way a shoe has been worn or cracked, the size or even the brand of shoe. "It was tough to get precise about the footprints because the snow wasn't that packed," Knight recalled. "Some snow had fallen into the prints, making it very difficult if not impossible to take footprint casts. So we took photographs instead."

Years later this decision would haunt the prosecution. Without casts, they were forced to rely on poor-quality photographs, most of which were fuzzy and difficult to read. The police later said that the plaster for footprint casts would have melted the snow and wouldn't have given an accurate reproduction.

Corporal Bielert recorded the footprints but didn't identify those of Kenny Gurba and the air officer. It would be of paramount concern to distinguish those footprints from the killers' footprints at the scene, and would later be seen as crucial in the eyes of the defence.

After the coroner pronounced the body dead at the scene, it was wrapped in blankets, put on a stretcher, and driven to St. Anthony's Hospital, where it would sit in a refrigerated coffin until someone could identify the girl.

Knight knew this wouldn't be easy. Even those who knew her, he thought, would have a difficult time recognizing her – she was that severely mangled. But he had to thank his stars for a restless curious kid.

"Lucky he went for a hunt for rabbit tracks or we wouldn't have found the body until spring or maybe not until ten years later and the trail would have been cold," Knight recalled. "By then the body would have been so badly decomposed, it would have been near impossible to identify it and all of the physical evidence would probably have been gone."

In the effort to identify the victim, officers hit the streets, yanked drunks and bartenders out of hotels, pulled teachers and kids out of the nearby schools, nabbed cab drivers from their shifts – anyone who might be able to offer a clue or identify the body. They chatted with prison guards trying to pick up scuttlebutt on the slaying.

While officers were busy looking for suspects, a worried Mrs. Patricia Benson had called the RCMP. A Native high-school student who roomed at her house hadn't come home the previous night. Mrs. Benson described a very petite, pretty girl, just over five feet tall. She wanted to file a missing person's report on Betty Osborne.

It couldn't be a coincidence. Twenty minutes after she made the call, the police asked Mrs. Benson and her husband, Bill, to come down to the morgue. She refused, saying she would only identify the clothing.

"They didn't insist and Bill went down instead," Mrs. Benson recalled. "I was too afraid and too upset. I felt terrible because I knew it must have been Betty." Shortly after, Bielert went to Betty's upstairs room in the small two-storey house. He took one of her notebooks and carefully treated the paper with silver nitrate to preserve any fingerprints.

Back at the morgue, Boyle and Knight were speculating. They had been out until 1:30 that morning investigating some thefts at the bush camps and had considered cruising by the pumphouse, a place where kids get up to no good. ''We said to hell with it,'' Boyle recalled. ''It was very cold and late and we figured it was kind of quiet. Maybe if we had stopped by we could have helped. But hindsight is 20-20.''

Boyle sat in the morgue as a steady stream of people came through, attempting to identify the body. But so far, no luck. When two ladies from the Indian residential school, Guy Hill, came in, thinking they might be able to identify the girl, they spotted Boyle wolfing down a hamburger.

''Doesn't this bother him?'' one of them asked another officer, seemingly surprised.

''I guess not, ma'am,'' the officer replied matter-of-factly.

Boyle hadn't eaten since the night before, and as the hours dragged on so had his appetite. Corpse or not, he was going to eat.

More people came through the morgue and still no luck. Boyle figured he'd better take the victim's boots off because they would be needed later as evidence. As he tugged at the thick, black, shiny rubber boots, gently pulling them off with her socks, he noticed a tattoo imprinted on the lower left leg: ''Cornelius Bighetty I Truly Love You! No Matter What.'' He immediately sent the police to question Bighetty – presumably the victim's lover.

Then they had another stroke of luck. The door slammed behind a gentleman in his early fifties. His name was Phillip McGillivary, a cab driver. ''He looked at the body and said: 'Look, I don't know who she is but I drove by the airport yesterday morning and saw this white or light blue car weaving on the road," Boyle recalled. "I thought I saw a newspaper or something like with red paint on it thrown out and I noticed the letters 42 on the plate," McGillivary had added.

What a break. "I really felt like I was doing some good police work when that fell into my lap," Boyle recalled. He quickly passed the information on to Grosenick.

The investigation started to move more quickly. Bielert came back to the morgue and the prints made a positive I.D. – the body was that of Helen Betty Osborne, treaty Indian 848.

Now came the most detested job – telling the victim's mother. "How do you tell a mother that her daughter was found mangled to death?" an officer asked.

After the autopsy was completed, police went back to Mrs. Benson's and gathered Betty's clothes, notebooks, albums, pens, pencils – whatever was in the small room where she'd lived and studied for three short months. They would take her body and belongings one hundred and forty miles east to Norway House Indian Reserve, and turn them over to Mrs. Justine Osborne and her husband Joe. Betty's belongings and memories of her boarding the plane for The Pas just a few short months ago were all they had left. "She couldn't stop sobbing, it was all pretty bad," Betty's brother, Isaiah recalled. "I had to leave, I couldn't handle it."

* * *

Sixteen years later, a ten-man, two-woman, all-white jury would convict one man of second-degree murder and sentence him to life imprisonment with no eligibility of parole for ten years. His appeal has recently been dismissed. A second man was acquitted, a third granted immunity from a charge of first-degree murder, and a fourth was never charged. A disgusted Mrs. Osborne stormed out of the courtroom, furious with the white justice system and the town that had shielded her daughter's killers for so long.

CHAPTER TWO

Betty wrapped her arms tightly around her mother, Justine, and promised to return to Norway House after graduation.

It was the summer of 1969 and it would be goodbye for almost a year. Justine had a hard time letting go of her first-born child. She didn't know much about The Pas, except that it could provide Betty with a high-school diploma – something kids from Norway House Indian Reserve couldn't get unless they left home. Most chose not to, but Betty was ambitious.

Her dream was to finish high school and go on to university. Betty, who was seventeen at the time, tossed around the idea of being a nurse, teacher or lawyer. But it was a little too early to plan; she would only be entering Grade 9 this year.

Like many teenagers in Norway House, Betty had outgrown the program at Roman Catholic Neckoway School and faced a choice between settling for a Grade 8 education or moving away from home to study further. Being the brightest and most studious of her family, she chose the latter and left under a new federal government program of integrating Indian students with whites. Betty chose The Pas over Thompson because she had a relative, Marion, who lived on the town reserve.

Leaving was tough on Betty's mother and her father, Joe, a fur trapper. Betty was the eldest and helped with the chores. She would clean up the house, babysit and help with the cooking. Taking care of ten kids was a tough job, especially in a place that didn't have electricity, running water or roads.

Part of Betty's responsibility was to look after her younger brothers and sisters: Billy, Kelvin, Douglas, Mark, Cynthia, Cecilia, Joe, and Tommy. It was a tough and tiring job. The second eldest, Isaiah, would haul water, and help with the more physically demanding chores. "She was so lovely," Justine recalled. "She used to always do everything that I told her and she used to be such a nice girl."

Justine let Betty go, somewhat reluctantly, at her daughter's insistence. At that time, Betty had already achieved more than half the Natives in Canada – she'd managed to finish elementary school. Only half of the Natives in the country would get a Grade 6 education. If she graduated from high school, she would be ahead of 97 per cent of the Native children in the Nation.

Betty would be staying at Guy Hill Indian Residential School, a Native residence at Clearwater Lake, but she wouldn't be attending there because it was a grade school. Instead, she'd take the bus twenty miles into The Pas each morning to the mostly white Margaret Barbour Collegiate. Since she didn't begin grade school until she was seven years old, she would be several years older than most of her Grade 9 classmates.

She would receive about a twenty-dollar monthly allowance from the federal Department of Indian Affairs and Northern Development. Her expenses, such as room and board and school supplies, would also be paid for by the government. It was all part of an Indian Affairs program designed to desegregate the schools by bussing in Indian kids from their remote reserves. Each school would get a fixed price for every Indian attracted to the classroom. But a good number of Native students would return home before the year was over because they were homesick and had difficulty studying in English.

Betty had been taught by priests at Neckoway and enjoyed school. One of her favourite subjects was mathematics, Isaiah recalled. "She liked school and didn't want to stop," he said. "She wanted to make something of herself and she was smart enough to do it." He said that Betty thought staying on the reserve would mean a life on welfare, like so many of the other families there. And for Betty, that wasn't good enough. "She wanted to work and have a family," Isaiah said.

That included having a comfortable home, a far cry from the one-room log cabin Betty's family of twelve had shared. "It was just like one giant bedroom with a stove in the middle," Isaiah recalled. The children and parents slept in the open room on wooden-frame beds.

One of her friends, Charlotte Swanson, said Betty would walk eight or nine miles a couple of times a week to visit her at Nelson River, the farthest end of Norway House reserve. "She told me she wanted to become what her family wasn't," Swanson remembered. Swanson, one of Betty's closest friends on the reserve, said Betty also talked about white men. "She couldn't understand why some Indian women liked white men when she didn't. I think it was because she thought they were physically kind of ugly," Swanson said. "She always said she would marry an Indian man."

Away from home, Betty would probably miss knowing each person's gesture and mannerisms, and hanging out at The Bay, a jaundiced yellow and green store on Rossville Island. It was the information depot of the community, where the news of gossip, births, deaths, and scandal cropped up. Isaiah said he and Betty would go there every day after school, and usually again after dinner.

There, the older women and men would relive and retell legends. Their talk would almost always revolve around the white man's injustices and Indians who had "gone white." It was something Betty had never considered. Born a Cree Indian on July 16, 1952, she wasn't about to sell out.

Norway House was home to 2,700 Metis, whites and Treaty Indians, many of them Cree like herself, many illiterate and unemployed. In Norway House, there was nothing to do; there was no reason to stay there, nor was there any reason to leave.

"Betty never really liked Norway House because she said there was nothing to do," Isaiah recalled. "It was really rough, then."

In Norway House, there was no industry or agriculture. The fish to be caught would feed only a few families. And there were too few animals left to make trapping a source of livelihood, except for the very best trappers, such as Betty's father, who was nicknamed King Trapper.

The rich history of Norway House as head of the western fur trade died almost a century ago. Back then, Norway House – it got its name from two Norwegian carpenters who first helped build it – was a booming frontier, a crossroads. All water routes to Hudson Bay from Alberta and Saskatchewan led there.

The reserve didn't produce anything but used to be a refuelling stop. People gradually settled near The Bay post. Boatmen and traders would retire and settle down or form casual relationships and father children. But all that ended when fur prices dropped. By the time the railway went through in the south, even the Hudson's Bay Company was cutting down its involvement in Norway House. Even as a youngster, Betty began to realize it was a reserve rich in history, but poor in everything else.

The reserve, which stretches ten miles south from Rossville down both sides of the Nelson River, includes two islands, Fort Island and Mission Island. The whites lived in white, yellow and turquoise buildings surrounded by fences perched on high promontories jutting into the river. Although there was nothing special about them, except for the view their location offered, they were highly visible and reserved exclusively for whites, almost all of whom were government, hospital or social services workers.

In stark contrast, Natives usually lived in brown and grey buildings, built perfectly to the dimensions of an Indian Affairs plan, except for the odd log house. They were segregated deep into the bush; all were uniform and small and most of them would deteriorate within twenty years, people said, because they were built so shabbily. Many of them had huge piles of firewood stacked alongside the house, for cooking and heating. The homes, almost all the same size and covered with the same monotonous whitewash, blended in with the bleak grey landscape.

Norway House's white people gave it a strong official air by wearing uniforms. Nurses wore white dresses and the doctors wore white jackets; priests and ministers wore black and nuns wore grey.

Betty's understanding of whites was based mostly on dealing with them in their roles as agents of business. If she was ill or had to pick up assistance, she'd meet with them; otherwise she didn't bother too much. To her, they were government. They ran the hospital nicknamed "the compound" on nearby Fort Island and lived near The Bay at Rossville. They treated sick babies and children – and there was an abundance of them.

White hospital workers complained that Indian women were slovenly and didn't clean their homes, making their children prone to disease. Such stereotyping stopped – at least temporarily – after a Native discovered in 1964 that the hospital's water supply was pumping in contaminated water from the Nelson River, making sick babies even more ill.

Back in the late 1960s a nurse was assigned to go into Native women's homes to try to teach them hygiene. She arrived bearing a bottle of disinfectant for each household. The nurse, waging a war against disease, would be on the lookout for children with rickets, impetigo, lice and coughs; oftentimes she would recruit her own patients.

Betty was one of those children who became very ill and had to stay in the hospital, a two-storey white clapboard building that had room for only the sickest of patients.

She almost died when she was thirteen, after eating some rotten beaver, her brother Isaiah recalled. "It was kind of scary for her."

Her fear came partly from remembering her baby brother's death from pneumonia in the late 1950s. Wallace died at the hospital. "The house was too cold and we couldn't keep it warm," Isaiah recalled. Many other Natives, some sick with malnutrition, tuberculosis, or venereal disease, feared going to the hospital and thought of it as a place to die, a morgue.

With the exception of the same cold, bitter winters and segregated housing for whites and Natives, The Pas didn't resemble Norway House. It was a big town – more than double the population of what Betty was used to – and it resembled what came closest to her idea of life in the fast lane. Betty, along with hundreds of other Native students, was thrust into The Pas during a time of economic explosion. It was a roaring, rich town, because of the growth of a massive pulp and paper mill then called Churchill Forest Industries.

The town's population of about 6,200, including about 460 Natives and Metis, couldn't accommodate this booming industry, which handed out as many jobs as there were people. Once word got out, transient workers from all over Canada came to The Pas in the 1960s looking for work in the forest industry. Some of them worked in bush camps deep in the wilderness. Even workers from Winnipeg, some 460 miles southeast, lined up to stake their fortune in the northern bush.

The money was rolling and so was the town. Downtown stores were swamped with business, as owners feverishly filled up racks of clothes; liquor stores doubled their orders of booze and beer, and the Gateway and Cambrian hotel bars lined up the hottest country and rock acts they could find. Everything that could make the rugged workers happy in The Pas could be found at those town bars, be it women, booze or drugs. They had the money and they loved to spend it.

The Pas, a bastardized Cree word meaning wooded narrows, was divided by the Saskatchewan River. Living on two Indian reserves and one Metis settlement on the north side of the river were about 1,200 people or about one-sixth of the town's population. Across the river, separated by a huge arched steel bridge, was the south side with the white residences and the shops, the hospital, government offices, churches and most of the schools – all run by whites.

The white part of The Pas, or the town side, was dumpy looking. It had a small post office, pool hall, legal aid building, drugstore, a couple of candy stores, a grocery store, Fishman's clothing store, a few bars, a bus and train station, and that's about it. Commonly referred to as the Gateway to the North, it nevertheless lacked the charm of many quaint small towns. For the most part, it was just plain ugly.

Many of the homes in The Pas were small aluminum-sided ones occupied by working class-families. The upper middle class consisted of the store owners and liquor-store managers. The gentry were the professionals, the judges, lawyers, and doctors. At the bottom of the social ladder were the Indians.

As far as most whites were concerned back then, The Pas Reserve was an eyesore on the way to Clearwater Lake; it could be seen clearly from Highway 10 north. It was just past the bridge, a clump of earth with tiny pastel-colored houses, many of them unkempt, which looked like they had been dropped at random from the sky. The whites didn't mind Big Eddy Reserve too much. Farther west and north of The Pas Reserve, it was neatly tucked deep into the bush, out of eyesight.

Outside of town was Clearwater Lake, a summer getaway lined with cottages about twenty miles northeast of The Pas. Clearwater Lake, dotted with jack pine and spruce trees, was a tranquil, soothing area – away from the noisy bustle of town. Cottages were abandoned during the cold-weather months, however: they had no running water or heat. It was a rather bleak place in the winter, virtually uninhabitable.

To the outsider, The Pas was the TV's idea of the wild wild west. It's where men were men, or rather, where white men were cowboys and Natives were Indians. Metis were Metis – until they hung around with whites. Then they were "apples" – red on the outside but white on the inside, Indians would say. Most whites considered Indians to be drunks. They thought them dirty and freeloaders of the system. Indians viewed whites as corrupt, untrustworthy and arrogant.

A 1965 study of Natives conducted by the Canadian Council of Christians and Jews found that almost 75 per cent of The Pas' residents showed some prejudice against Indians and 10 per cent showed extreme prejudice. A majority of people stated that Indians were shiftless, undependable. Nearly half the people agreed with the statements that, "The homes of people of Indian descent offer nothing good to a child or elderly person," that "Most people of Indian descent show complete disregard for the common standards of personal decency," and that Indian children tended to be illegitimate.

Only sex and booze connected the Native man's world with that of the white, and then only after dark. Perhaps a Native woman and drunken white man would meet in a flophouse around the corner from the Gateway Hotel. Or fights would break out between Natives and whites in a dimly lit hotel. They began simply enough; a Native man would size up a white man's woman, or simply look at a white man the wrong way. Presumably, there was no right way for an Indian to look at a white man.

As much as the whites moaned about the Indians, however, they were perfectly content to sell them overpriced bootleg liquor at the Nip House and second-rate clothing in the stores, and charge the drunken ones up to triple the normal cab fare for the five-mile ride back to The Pas Reserve.

RCMP stationed in The Pas had one of the toughest

towns to police. A local motorcycle gang, dubbed The Pas Bikers, a group of tough-talking teenagers, didn't help any. They were a tightly knit group of about ten to fifteen long-haired, long-bearded teenagers on the verge of turning into men; but slowly. They were too small in numbers and too unorganized to be a criminal association like some motorcycle gangs. Still, they asserted their power through intimidation, physical violence, foul language, and threats.

Every weekend there was a brawl at the Gateway or the Cambrian, fights among Natives and whites, Natives and Metis, Natives and bikers, or whites and whites. Cops worked long, hard hours policing the streets, working on manslaughters, homicides, countless cases of break-and-enter, thefts, and suspicious drownings. As early as 1968, police could count on forty-five arrests a night each weekend. RCMP officers worked four to five hours overtime daily. Teenage vandalism was becoming a growing problem, too, with parents attending meetings in droves trying to figure out how to stop kids from breaking home and car windows.

Downtown stores couldn't get their insurance renewed because their display windows had been smashed so often. You could walk for blocks down Fisher Avenue, the main drag of The Pas, and not see one window that hadn't been broken or cracked.

The town's jail had only four cells and when the fighting and drinking was at its heaviest, the men were housed in a twenty-five-bed dormitory. The regular weekend brawls were so predictably rough that RCMP Assistant Commissioner W.G. Mudge warned The Pas town council in 1970 that unless the community paid for more officers, the force might not renew its contract that June. His tactic worked; in less than a year the number of constables in the rural and town detachments increased from eight to twelve.

Mayor Harry Trager of The Pas said weekend brawls and street fights were the product of immigrant mill and bush workers from more than half a dozen European countries, who didn't speak English well. "It's the transients . . . the workers from nearby construction projects who pour into town every weekend," he told newspapers at the time. "Most of them don't have anywhere to go and they hang around the main street all night. With all the excessive drinking, it doesn't take long for the fights to start."

Racial unrest in The Pas would reach a crescendo in April 1975, with a wild encounter involving 350 Indians and whites that nearly erupted into a full-scale race riot outside the Gateway Hotel. The Pas Bikers and The Saxons from Thompson had forced their way into the New Avenue Hotel on Fisher Avenue with home-made weapons, shotguns, baseball bats, axe handles, metal pipes, and hockey sticks. Shortly afterwards, they left for the Gateway Hotel. Hotel staff locked all doors and advised the patrons – Indians and Metis – to remain inside until the RCMP could disperse the mob. When the bikers and some juveniles were denied entrance into the Gateway, they muttered, "Fuck this, let's go clean house," one resident at the scene recalled. A hotel owner was quoted as saying that the bikers and a number of followers "rode in aiming to cause trouble for any group of Indians they could find."

The mob hurled rocks and bottles through the hotel's windows and several frightened patrons took to the floor for cover. But many of the Metis and Indians inside were reportedly ready for a fight and held out until about 4:00 A.M. That's when the fight moved into the parking lot and the Indian and Metis handed bikers "a good licking," according to newspaper reports.

Only three Mounties were on duty when the disturbance broke out, but nine off-duty police were summoned later. Still, "We didn't really have enough people to break up something like this," one Mountie was quoted as saying. "It is just a matter of playing it cool and hoping for the best." Since police couldn't battle the mob, they

activated the town's fire alarm and members of the vol-
unteer brigade stood by ready to hose down the crowd,
but it had already broken up by then. A school bus from
The Pas Reserve later took many of the Native patrons
safely back to the reserve.

The brawl resulted in $4,000 damage to the Gateway.
Police arrested about forty people, including a number
of juveniles, on such charges as carrying offensive weapons, assaulting police, and creating a disturbance in a
public place. Weekend brawls became more subdued
after the near-riot, but other problems emerged. The Pas
Reserve built its own $8.2 million, fifteen-business mall
in 1976, two years after a group of white merchants
attempted to block in court the construction of Canada's
first Indian-owned and -operated shopping centre. The
merchants had argued that the shopping centre would
violate the Indian Act and an 1875 treaty, which would
have made expenditure of public funds on the shopping
centre illegal. They also said the mall would destroy the
town's commercial base. The Federal Court of Canada
rejected the merchants' case in 1974 and construction of
the centre continued with money borrowed from private
sources, but guaranteed by the federal government. When
the Otineka Mall opened in October 1976, an economic
war surfaced between whites and natives as they battled
for customers.

* * *

Unlike in Norway House, daily contact with white people
couldn't be avoided in The Pas. White students would
be sitting next to Betty in the classroom. ''There was a
fair amount of animosity between the older white and
Indian kids,'' Margaret Barbour teacher Vel McAdam
recalled. ''Integration was a good idea but a lot of [Na-
tive] kids didn't want to come and there were a lot of
[white] parents who were resentful of these kids who
were getting their way paid.''

Margaret Barbour Collegiate wasn't prepared for racial
integration. Teachers would complain, some quite ac-

curately, that Native children didn't know how to work. At some northern reserves where there was little to do Natives have learned quite successfully how to manage their time through ritualized inactivity. Performing simple household chores, such as fetching water or looking after the children, was done in the least time-efficient way – it's a method of dealing with too much time. Children would never see their parents study, read, or even care too much about school. Parents never seemed to pay much attention to the clock, so how on earth were their kids supposed to know how to crack the books every night? Betty was unusual in this respect and seemed to enjoy school work. While her mother could read, her father couldn't, Isaiah recalled. Both of her parents spoke English as well as Cree, but neither they nor her brothers or sisters were very studious, he said.

Another big problem was the English language and the teaching of subjects that were useless, at least as far as the inherently practical Indians were concerned. How was the learning of poetry and teaching of algebra going to help an Indian find a job? Native students, despite being thrust into the midst of strangers, a new culture and classes held in a second language, were somehow expected to perform like their white counterparts. Even the mayor at the time condemned the policy of integration before it began, saying the Indians weren't ready for it yet. It was doomed for failure.

Betty didn't trust white people and, in fact, was afraid of them. To her, The Pas resembled every cowboy and Indian movie she had seen back at her home in Norway House. It was a wild town, with a voracious appetite for booze and sex. To her, Betty's friends recalled, whites seemed violent, confrontational. Natives were merely the bull's-eye in a town dartboard.

Other things bothered her too. She complained of the white people's terrible eating habits and their food – they ate such things as pork and canned foods. Betty liked moose, beaver, fresh fish, and her traditional bannock, a paste with the consistency of bread, made with flour, baking powder, and lard.

As much of a struggle it was to master the English language, Betty quickly settled in and grew to like school, but she remained introverted and shy with whites. It was her Native friends she would open up to. She became part of a tightly knit group of about twenty kids, most of them Treaty Indians. Friends described her as strong-willed, bright, and humorous, someone who knew how to have fun. While she was a studious girl, she would drink with friends on the weekends and liked having a boyfriend.

It was important for Native students to stick together. They had things in common, including homesickness and a desire to do well in life; it gave them a feeling of belonging.

Most of Betty's week nights were spent studying but that year she also met Cornelius Bighetty, a man who would become a very significant part of her life when she returned in the fall for Grade 10.

It was the end of June and it was time to go home. Betty excitedly flashed her report card reading ''pass'' and ''satisfactory'' around Norway House. Betty became a success story on the reserve and the gossip at The Bay was now how she would come back a teacher one day.

Isaiah recalled spending summers with Betty. ''We would ask my mom for some money and then take the boat across the river and go drinking,'' he recalled. Like many teenagers, Betty and Isaiah began experimenting with alcohol. He said one of the difficulties getting booze back then, though, was that the bar and vendor outside of Norway House would only sell it to whites or Metis, but not to Natives. ''We would always have to pay some-one Metis to go in there and get it for us,'' he recalled.

But it was also a period of difficult times for the Os-borne family. Justine, fed up with Joe spending so much time away from home trapping, had begun drinking heav-ily, and eventually moved in with another man, Jimmy

Osborne – no relation to her husband. (Isaiah said she moved around the New Year of 1970 but wasn't interested in taking any of her children with her.) As soon as Isaiah got word that a man had stolen his mother away from him and the others, he went over to Jimmy's to tell him off. "I beat him up and every time I saw him I kept beating him up because he was with my mother," Isaiah recalled.

Betty's father, Joe, was away trapping, so "Most of us were taken by my [maternal] grandmother up in Cross Lake," Isaiah recalled. "But we felt like nobody cared about us, that nobody wanted us." He didn't live at his grandmother's home for very long and was eventually put into a foster home because of repeated thefts.

Betty took the news hard about her parents splitting up. "She was close to my mother and my father," Isaiah explained. Betty told her friend Charlotte about her disapproval of her mother's drinking and new relationship. "She was mad at her mother for taking off like that," Charlotte recalled. Betty wanted to return to school but she also knew that if she wanted to come home, she had nowhere to stay, except with her grandmother, Ida McKay, who was already taking care of most of Justine's children, the youngest of whom was only two.

Betty went back to the residential school, unpacked her bags, and settled in to a general program at Margaret Barbour Collegiate. It offered a program many Native kids were streamed into, one step up from vocational school and a step down from the regular curriculum. It would qualify her to attend community college, not university.

Betty spent more and more time with Cornelius Bighetty. He was a couple of years younger than she but he shared her striving for direction in life; he planned to go to Brandon University about 120 miles west of Winnipeg, take political science and then go back home to his reserve, Pukatawagan, a 150-mile train ride north from The Pas.

Standing slightly over six feet, he towered over Betty's

five-foot, one-inch frame. He was strong and handsome and just about every Indian girl would gather at the familiar hangout, the Indian Affairs office, and watch him play cards or ping-pong, just to get close to him. It took several months of buddying around, and dozens of card games at the Indian Affairs building before Betty became Cornelius's girlfriend. She shared that status with three or four other women, but she accepted it. She knew he was too young to settle down. But when that time came, she would be there with open arms, ready to make a happy, married life with him.

Betty knew not to go with other boys because Cornelius, like most Indian men, wouldn't put up with it. There had been other boyfriends for Betty, most of them at the Reserve, but none were like Cornelius. Indian women fit to marry couldn't be seen having more than one lover at a time and could never go out with white boys – that would make them less than an Indian in the men's eyes. It was something Betty never did. Each time she made love to Cornelius she pretended she was the only one and Cornelius thought she believed it, too. Betty never mentioned a word to him about his other girlfriends, except when she confided in his brother, Pascall, or Cornelius's father, Baptiste. Just about every weekend Betty took the train with Cornelius to visit his relatives in Pukatawagan, a Cree word meaning fishing place, more commonly referred to as "Puk."

Cornelius's father took an immediate liking to Betty. She was pretty, domestic, traditional, very pleasant and rarely travelled without her black-beaded rosary. She wasn't like those other "bitchy" Indian women who complained about the lack of conveniences at Puk.

There was no electricity, no running water, and no heat, except for that from a wooden stove. Dinners were spent eating by the light of a coal oil lamp or candles. But it didn't bother Betty; in fact she quite liked it because it was so much like her home. In the centre of the one-room log house in Norway House was a huge wood stove, used for cooking and heating. Only the violence – Puk's alarming homicide rate – disturbed her. Indians would get wild with drink and fire shotguns at people on the roadway. "You'd be walking and someone would shoot at you out of nowhere," Pascall recalled. And there would be times when Cornelius came home drunk, beaten and bleeding.

Most times, Cornelius would down so many beers on those weekend visits he would pass out on the couch, his legs and arms hanging in every direction, mouth gaping open. Betty and Baptiste would glance over at him and laugh. She would explain to Baptiste that she didn't care too much for drinking, except on weekends with her girlfriends.

Betty tried to make a good impression on Baptiste, as with other elders, by saying the right things. But she was like most teenagers and tended to drink quite heavily on weekends. Jail guards in The Pas remember Betty getting so drunk in bars that she, like many other Native girls, was housed in a prison cell a couple of times to sober up.

On the weekend visits to Puk, Betty, and Baptiste would play cards until all hours of the night, chatting about school. Betty daydreamed about what a wonderful husband Cornelius would be, especially if he stopped his drinking. Baptiste would make fun of Betty's Swampy Cree dialect, and she, of course, would tell him his Woodlands Cree was charming, even though she found it hard to understand at times.

Baptiste was a traditional Puk man. He believed that if a woman and man planned to marry, they should first have a trial marriage of one or two years. He encouraged his sons to bring their girlfriends home for weekend visits. It was practical and seemed to work well. Baptiste was also Betty's biggest cheerleader and hoped that one day she would be Cornelius's wife. Of course, Cornelius listened more to his practical mother, Cecile, who told him to get an education first and worry about settling down later.

Betty couldn't help but make a good impression on Cecile. She always offered to do the dishes, sweep the floor and help cook whenever she visited. And Cornelius's brother, Pascall, also cared for Betty. She was vulnerable, he said, remembering the time she had told them over dinner that she was afraid of white people and how she tried to stay away from them in The Pas. "It was almost as if she had a premonition about them," Pascall recalled.

During those weekend visits Betty would talk about missing Norway House. As much as she knew there could be no future for her there, she grew homesick and missed her family. But she made a commitment to persevere. She knew that a fair number of kids in her class had quit the previous schoolyear and gone home, mostly because they were homesick. Even her brother Billy, three years her junior, had gone to school at Guy Hill Indian Residential School in The Pas only to quit after a very short time. Being with Cornelius was a big comfort and gave her the direction she needed.

But Grade 10 wasn't going so well for Betty. By the end of the year she had earned only two out of eight credits. That was poor compared to the usual course load but was average for most Indian kids. Being homesick was part of Betty's problem but the biggest stumbling blocks, as for most Native kids, were the cultural differences and the language barrier. Many felt they didn't belong and weren't wanted.

Betty spent that summer after Grade 10 at Norway House, spending a lot of time with her friend Charlotte, who, years later, would marry Betty's brother Isaiah. In the fall of 1971, Betty took one last walk to Charlotte's parents' home in Nelson River and asked if she could borrow her prescription brown-rimmed glasses for class because she had to strain her eyes to see the board. She promised to return them at Christmas, the next time she would be visiting. Isaiah and Betty's father, Joe, saw her off at the airport at Norway House and waved goodbye as the small white wings of the plane shook in the windy air.

When Betty went back to school she had no choice but to do Grade 10 over again. Now nineteen, she knew she would be at least twenty-one when she graduated. That year she decided to board with a white family in town. It was something new the school was trying; desegregation, they thought, would be much easier if the Indian kids lived with whites. It would help them adjust and be a good influence on many of the Indian kids who, some thought, came from sub-standard, dirty homes.

Mrs. Patricia Benson took the posted notice off the bulletin board at Margaret Barbour Collegiate and decided to take Betty into her home at 441 Lathlin Avenue. The Department of Indian Affairs would give Mrs. Benson an allowance to board her. Mrs. Benson and her husband, Bill, had never taken in any Native kids as boarders but thought it might be pleasant to take in Betty and another girl, Muriel Robinson; the two would be good company for their three young children. As much as Betty was wary of whites, she thought living with the Bensons would be good for her and the Bensons' home was only a two-minute walk from school, close to all of the shops and the movie theatre right in town.

Living on the south side of the Saskatchewan River – the white side – was tough for Betty. At least over on the north side of the river she had the Big Eddy and The Pas reserves and Umpherville settlement to give her a feeling of belonging; that was clearly Indian and Metis turf. But she felt a little better knowing there were other Indian kids boarding with white families and at least she would be living with another Native girl. Muriel was from Cross Lake Reserve.

While she was always polite, Betty didn't mix with white kids much and didn't get involved in many school activities. Even though she had been a good volleyball player at school in Norway House, Betty wouldn't play the sport in The Pas. "She said she didn't want to wear shorts because she didn't like showing her legs," Cornelius recalled. "She was very shy that way." Instead, she went to watch Cornelius play volleyball and basketball.

A lot of Indian kids didn't play on school teams so almost all of the teams were exclusively white. But Cornelius organized his own team of Indian kids, which played so well that white kids would sometimes hang around and join in informally. One of those was an eighteen-year-old named Lee Colgan. He would be charged with Betty's murder fifteen years later.

On the weekends she didn't go to Puk she would baby-sit Mrs. Benson's three children or go to the movies with Cornelius and a few of their friends. They sat on the left side of the movie theatre – the only seats Indians were allowed to take. Otherwise they ran the risk of being kicked out or the usher would make a point of embarrassing them by loudly directing them to the other side, to the sneers of most whites.

There had also been instances of overt racism directed at Betty and most other Indian girls and boys. Whether Betty walked with one girlfriend, male friends, or alone, she would sometimes be called "fucking squaw," "dirty Indian whore," "potato" or be told "the only good Indian is a dead Indian." People would spit at her and mistake her for some of the loose Indian women who hung out at the Gateway Hotel.

Sometimes Betty, hair in a shag and teased up on top, was mistaken for an "Edwards Avenue girl" – an Indian or Metis girl, who, for a couple of glasses of beer, would go along with any man as long as he wanted her. Betty wouldn't.

* * *

It was Friday, November 12, 1971. At about 8:00 P.M. Betty went with her friend George Ross, sixteen, also from Norway House, to visit a friend in the hospital.

After that, the two stopped off at a convenience store in The Pas from where she called Mrs. Benson to ask if she could bring him home for a visit. Mrs. Benson said yes.

They trudged along in the snow on that dark night and went to her home, where they started drinking beer in the kitchen. Mrs. Benson walked by on the way into the livingroom and spotted the pair drinking. ''That's enough now,'' Mrs. Benson recalled saying. She ordered George out. Betty followed, saying she wanted to go uptown to buy a bottle of Coke and a bag of chips and settle in to watch the late movie when she came back.

Mrs. Benson gave Betty permission to go to the store providing she would come back right away. It was very cold, and at night The Pas became wild, hardly a place a young girl would want to roam about. Betty threw on her jacket, blue gloves and black rubber boots and walked with George uptown.

But as Betty and George were walking, they spotted three friends, including Eva Simpson and Marion Osborne. They stopped off at a vendor and picked up a 24-bottle case of beer, then they returned to Mrs. Benson's. They went to the small back shed to drink, without her permission.

After a few drinks, Betty was kind of drunk, Ross said, and the five of them walked uptown. That's when Betty bumped into Lillian Michelle with Cornelius in the lobby of the Cambrian Hotel. Betty was furious and began arguing and fighting with Lillian over her man. The argument became so heated that Cornelius had to separate the two screaming women, who were yanking each other's hair.

After that, George went home. He last saw Betty upset, sad and without Cornelius, walking along Edwards Avenue near the railroad tracks at ll:30 P.M., in the direction of home. She never made it.

CHAPTER THREE

"I know you've ripped us off for $900 and you're going to pay it back," Art Fishman recalled saying. Lee Colgan signed a statement in his boss's office, agreeing to pay $25 a week from his pay cheques. Once he had paid those instalments, he would have to quit.

It was 1971 and Lee was seventeen. He'd been working at Fishman's, the downtown clothing store, as a part-time sales clerk, stockboy, and cashier after school and on Saturdays – his first steady job. Mr. Fishman, the owner, had hired Lee because he knew his family. Lee's father, Harold "Bud" Colgan, was the manager of a Manitoba Liquor Control Commission store. Meek and mild, he was a well-respected member of the community. He was responsible, efficient and seemed an honorable man, and that's what Mr. Fishman expected to get when he hired Lee.

One of the things he got was a darned good salesman. When Lee put his mind to it he could sell anything to anybody – whether they wanted it or not. Mr. Fishman was very happy with Lee and considered him to be a good employee in the beginning. He was sharp, fast, and seemed sincere. Men would come into Fishman's to buy a pair of pants and end up leaving with bags stuffed full of shirts, shoes, and belts. Lee was taught the skills of a salesman – to be courteous and pleasant, and to believe that every customer who walked through Fishman's wanted to buy something. And Lee was prepared to sell it.

His first few months were among the store's busiest times in its fifty-two years of business. Fishman's moved to a bigger and better location, expanding its lines of clothing and paying off the renovations in one year – a result of the town's boom. Churchill Forest Industries had exploded with work and new settlers were coming into town with fists full of cash, eager to spend. "The town went wild – there was money galore," Mr. Fishman recalled. "People were making and spending big money."

Around that time, Mr. Fishman noticed his cash was coming up short every night. He carefully recorded the amount of money missing and estimated that over a period of months he'd lost about $900. He couldn't figure out where this money was going, so he started making subtle enquiries among the staff. An employee informed Mr. Fishman that Lee had come into a lot of cash recently and was blowing it on booze every weekend, going on big drinking bouts. After a brief meeting in Mr. Fishman's office, both agreed to settle it informally. After all, there was no need to involve Lee's parents or call the police – gossip about that would spread like wildfire in such a small town.

At an early age, Lee had begun paving the road to a life of booze and pills. He was drunk for days, months, even years at a time. Alcoholism is one of the North's biggest problems. Since there was nothing much to do north of the 53rd parallel, mainly because of its geographical isolation, many young people would drink. At seventeen, Lee was a self-described weekend drunk. He had first started experimenting with marijuana in 1970. Later, he would graduate to harder drugs such as LSD, MDA, mescalin, and blotter acid.

The brother of Judy, Richard, and Randal, Lee must have been a constant disappointment to his father and mother, who was a church pianist and music teacher. As a teenager, he was known for his temper tantrums, a troubled young man who had great difficulty trying to hold down a steady job. If things didn't go Lee's way, he would scream and become a ''mentally erratic boy,'' Mr. Fishman recalled. ''He was totally unpredictable. For the last few months he worked here, you couldn't tell from one day to the next what he was going to be like. He just couldn't take pressure, especially when we were busy.''

Some people who knew Lee said his mother, Joyce, was an overbearing, domineering woman who took out her miseries on him by ordering him to do chores around the house. Others said she was trying to discipline a spoiled, young man who insisted on being waited on hand and foot. Despite those faults, Lee's parents would always come to him in a moment of need. They truly loved their boy and desperately wanted him to make something of himself.

Even so, Lee would complain to employees at Fishman's that his mother was always making him do mundane household chores such as cleaning the toilet and washing the dishes. It must have really bothered Lee to do these chores; he was always griping about them and quickly earned himself the reputation of being a whiner.

Like many of his peers, Lee attended Margaret Barbour Collegiate in The Pas. To the teachers he appeared bright but at times preoccupied. When he set himself a task, he would do a project thoroughly and well, but if he wasn't that interested, it would be virtually impossible to hold his attention. Overall, teachers remembered Lee for getting average-to-good grades. At times, Lee could be quite frustrating to those who only wanted to help him.

As the son of a high-profile figure in town with a good government job, Lee was always being watched and talked about. Townspeople kept waiting for him to follow in his father's footsteps, or to at least make something of himself. They kept waiting. Still, back in 1971 there was nothing too unusual about Lee's heavy drinking. Teen-

agers went on drinking binges regularly; the legal age
dropped in September 1970 from twenty-one to eighteen,
and they had a lot of catching up to do. Boys would cram
into their fathers' late-model Chryslers and Fords on Friday and Saturday nights, cruise along Fisher Avenue,
blow a few joints, and look for a good time. In The Pas,
there wasn't much else to do except shoot the odd game
of pool, and go dancing at the Royal Canadian Legion
or drinking.

Lee often borrowed his father's 1967 two-door white
Chrysler Newport on weekends to go cruising, usually
with his close friend Jim Houghton, who lived right across
the road from Lee on Constant Avenue, and Norman
Manger. Sometimes they pulled up on the side of the
road and put their heads out the windows to chat up girls,
inviting them along to small parties where they were the
only guests. But many of the girls, having seen it all
before, knew better and waved off their crude advances.

Other times the three would shoot a few games of pool
or hang out at the Gateway, guzzle a few beers, and then
crash a late-night party. If there weren't any, they would
go to the Nip House, an after-hours bootlegging joint and
hangout.

Lee would often go to midnight weekend dances at the
Royal Canadian Legion, where he would briefly chat with
Cornelius Bighetty, a schoolmate. "He was in my class
and a good friend of mine," Cornelius recalled. "Betty
and I would bump into him frequently, usually when I
played volleyball or when we went to school dances."

Betty probably wouldn't have paid much attention to
Lee Colgan. After all, he was a white kid and Cornelius's
friend, not hers. She might have recalled him, though,
when she went into Fishman's, usually to cash her allowance cheques.

Fortified booze, sunshine acid, blotter acid, hashish,
marijuana – you name it; people said it was at the Gateway. Any hour of the day, any day of the week. Women
– short, tall, fat, skinny, white or brown – could be found

Jim Houghton (photo: Brian E. Roque)

Lee Colgan (photo: Brian E. Roque)

clustered giggling and drinking in corners. They were invisible until midnight. Then, cigarette smoke streaming into the air, their wafting perfume attracted smiling, free-spending men, ready to cater to their every whim, at least for an hour or two.

Lee often attempted to pick up women at the Gateway, admittedly without much luck. Despite his fresh-faced look, he wasn't very successful at attracting girls to form a steady relationship either. He was above average in height and athletic, and had soft brown hair, pointed, strong features, and wide eyes. Only occasionally would the guys see Lee with a girl on his arm and, more often than not, that girl was Native.

In many ways, Lee was the opposite to his easy-going friend Jim "Smiley" Houghton, even though they both came from very similar backgrounds. The son of Margaret and Frank Houghton, a meat-packing salesman, Jim was the leader of his five or six close friends and was looked up to by his two sisters, Donna and Diane.

In 1971, Jim, at twenty-three, was reasonably handsome and had been going out with Shannon White, who would eventually become his wife, since his teens.

He was nicknamed Smiley because he seemed like such a happy, gentle fellow, who was always laughing and making jokes. Jim was always considered the tougher, smarter guy among the crowd. He was the clever one who did well in his physics classes in high school, the athletic guy who played golf and baseball and curled. If you were ever in a jam, Jim could get you out of it. According to several of his friends, he was a character with all the ingredients to be the most likely to succeed of the group.

He came from what appeared to the perfect, middle-class family. The Houghtons lived directly across the street from the Colgans on the south side of town. They were a happy family, spending their summers at the cottage on Clearwater Lake, just like the Colgans. They were proud too, and it showed. The family name was spelled out in red plastic letters a foot high on the roof of their chocolate-brown cottage, which was secluded by jack pine trees and water.

Jim was a pleasant-looking guy, with dirty blonde hair and deep brown, close-set eyes; small, upturned features; and a wide, happy smile. Although he was average in height, he was large and stocky, giving the impression he could take care of himself. Some say he was nearly as handsome as his father, Frank, a veritable lady-killer if he wanted to be. And Jim was, at times, too. When he and Lee teamed up on their drives east to Cormorant and north to Wanless, heavily Native-populated areas, they would rarely leave without finding a good party with girls. But talk of those parties would be reserved exclusively for the guys at the bar over a cold brew, not for the women they might be dating.

Jim was admired by his friends for his perseverance and stubbornness. It was something that helped him overcome his disability, a club foot. On and off for years, Jim wore a waist-high cast, following operations to make his legs the same length. To his friends, Jim was a fighter. No disability was going to stop him from joining in sports and, in fact, he succeeded quite well at them. "The only time it really bothered him was at hockey because he couldn't skate like the rest of the guys," one of his friends recalled. "But he never complained about it."

According to his friends, Jim was very good at hiding things that bothered him. Jim seemed to be a selfless, humble guy – the type of man that didn't want to bother you with his troubles. After all, he was more than capable of dealing with them on his own. Only his older sister, Donna, knew how Jim would brood inside. "On the outside he would seem happy and calm enough but on the inside he would be sad, nervous, or very worried, depending on the situation," Donna recalled. "He kept his feelings inside."

Only when Jim had had a few beers did he show a different side, which only a few select friends saw. They describe how he would go "haywire," and become a beer-guzzling, back-slapping, wildly extroverted man. Jim lived up to the image in the classic country-and-western song: he was a fast-drivin', heavy-drinkin', hard-lovin' man who lived with intensity, a tough talker who got into the odd scrap.

In his youth, Jim was a jack of all trades. He worked at the sawmill or on hydro projects, and helped manage a fruit store in Thompson. He was cool and collected but friendly, and had a good sense of humour. His posture spoke of confidence; he walked casually in his tan-colored cowboy boots, standing with his thumb hitched into the top of his faded blue jeans with its shining metal buckle. He undid the top two buttons of his pastel shirts, but not enough so you could see his round belly. Hardly anyone could find a bad word to say about him; he was almost too nice, too perfect.

The group also included Norman Bernard Manger, a tall, lanky fellow who'd had a very sad life. His mother had died when he was young and his father, a carpenter by trade, was a frail old man who had a tendency to drink excessively, leaving little time to raise his three sons and daughter.

So Norm had to fend for himself. In 1971, he was twenty-five. He was lonely and desperate for a place to sleep. He would take his weary body, limp with alcohol, and curl up under porches or sleep on the floor or benches at all-night laundromats. When he was lucky he would crash on the floor of his friends' homes.

The better half of his days were spent drinking and looking for places to sleep. Sometimes he would take the odd menial job – anything he could find to earn enough money to keep himself fed and stocked in beer and wine. At one time he worked in the mill at Churchill Forest Industries bleaching wood. But for the most part, Norm led a monotonous life of drinking. He was almost invisible in The Pas.

It's no wonder he became cynical about life at a very

early age. Even in high school, Norm was described as withdrawn and introverted, but also very bright – even calculating at times. Even though he was tall, strong, and athletic during his Margaret Barbour Collegiate days, it wasn't long before he became consumed by drink.

By most accounts, he was a boy who had not been loved, who had never known the affection of a mother, father, or woman. There was no one there to heal his wounds, to encourage him, or even to care about him. The word family meant nothing to Norm; his parents were alcoholics, his sister moved away to Hamilton, Ontario, and one of his brothers, Jim, had a severe drinking problem and committed suicide some years later. Norm's life, for the most part, was depressing and largely uneventful – or so everyone thought.

Norm, like Jim and Lee, lived during the biggest boom The Pas had known in decades. But Norm usually celebrated in solitude. Even when he went out with friends, he didn't speak much. Instead, he would lean against the railing of the New Avenue Hotel, guzzling wine and sucking back the wafts of marijuana floating through the room, slowly slipping into dreamland.

Norm didn't lead the extroverted, fun-loving life of the men from the big mines up north. He wasn't like the bush camp workers who lived for the Friday five o'clock bell to ring at Churchill Forest Industries, either.

His life instead was the male equivalent of that led by downtrodden Native women who wandered dazed through the streets. Although Norm was white, he had all the physical markings and many of the mannerisms of an Indian. He had thick, shiny black hair, dark skin, high cheekbones, deep brown eyes, and constantly looked down at the ground when spoken to. The homeless Native women shared the same despair Norm did.

Several Native women hung out on the streets and at the Gateway and Cambrian hotels. They were waifs who had been turned out onto the street either because their parents didn't want them or because they cost too much to feed. They were neither beautiful nor attractive. They craved affection in any form, and often that was provided by the sex-starved men that came south to The Pas from the northern mining camps.

They were malnourished, with dried eyes, prematurely wrinkled faces, and round bellies due to starchy diets of bannock. Sometimes they wore black or green army pants, black nylon jackets, and black tops. They stood leaning sloppily to one side. Some of them sniffed glue to get over the beating from the night before, but all were helpless because they had nowhere to sleep except under the railroad bridge and nowhere to work, except maybe at the Gateway. Some of them would settle for a glass of beer from any man who cared to offer one, hoping to find a warm place at the end of night, whether it was the flophouse around the corner from The Gateway or the back seat of a car.

Most men took these women in until they grew tired of them; some men took them in out of pity. Except for the older, married men, some who frequented the Gateway preferred them to white women. They would do just about anything to please the men and didn't pester them about having a relationship. Nor did they want to go anywhere special, or to even meet their friends.

The bikers, however, weren't likely to pick up Native girls. To them, "squaws" were second-grade and infested with sexually transmitted diseases; they were loose and only for desperate men who couldn't get anything better. Bikers, the non-conformists in town, hung out at the Gateway and Cambrian hotels. Some had girlfriends, who were usually young and pretty and whose fathers were up in arms over their no-good boyfriends.

Outsiders called them The Pas Bikers but they didn't go by any particular name themselves. They were a closely knit group of about ten to fifteen guys who considered themselves members of a cool, private brotherhood. Whatever their name, they were always found in the midst of the brawls at the Gateway. Oftentimes they were

Dwayne Johnston (photo: Brian E. Roque)

Norm Manger (photo: Lisa Priest)

blamed by police for starting them. As much as they probably would have liked to have taken credit for the fights, they weren't always the instigators.

When the cops zoomed into the Gateway with the paddy wagon, the bikers were the first to be thrown into it, and the first to get out. They'd kick out the back door with their feet and run off as the police were following. The police would often catch the escapees half-way home and throw them in jail. They were the rebels who only wanted to live the laws of the wild-wild west.

But the town's problems of alcoholism and routine brawls didn't arise because of the tension between Natives, Métis, and whites. It began in the mid-1960s when Duff Roblin's Progressive Conservative government decided what this economically depressed community needed was a thriving industry. So in 1969, Churchill Forest Industries (CFI) began the first phase of a planned $1,000,000 complex. When the logging industry arrived after years of slow growth in the mellow farm society of the Carrot River Valley, the town went wild. A town that had only known winter trapping, fabulous fishing, and the search for precious metals was now swept away by the mills.

The Pas Bikers, many of whom worked in the mill at CFI, were no exception but their excitement consisted of occasionally hanging out with The Saxons, a biker gang from Thompson.

Bikers wore what cops called "shitkicker boots," those big, black-leather, heavy-soled, calf-high boots with square steel toes. They perfectly matched the black leather jackets, the faded, torn blue jeans, and the Harley-Davidsons. Their faces were buried underneath long hair and scraggly unkempt beards, two eyes peering into a beer glass, similar to the seemingly uncivilized and untamed mountain men.

Dwayne Archie Johnston was one of them. He was born on June 7, 1953, the blond, blue-eyed son of Marie and Willard Johnston, in the tiny northern Ontario town of Geraldton. His parents moved to The Pas and then separated when the children – two boys and two girls – were very young, leaving Dwayne with his mother. Dwayne attended Margaret Barbour Collegiate and got his first job in Grade 9 with CFI. In 1970, he found work at Canadian National Railways as a brakeman, eventually dropping out of school because he couldn't do both full-time.

Dwayne Johnston was a character of many contrasts. He had the capacity to be very loving but only to those who were loyal to him. To those who weren't he could be quite cruel, at least verbally. He could show surprising common sense, yet he'd do stupid things. He had no time for anyone who didn't share his interest in bikes. If people couldn't talk about choppers, motorcycle engines, or various mechanical problems, he'd exclude them from the conversation.

One thing stands out about Dwayne: although he enjoyed the collective brotherhood of motorcycle gangs, he was a loner, an outsider who'd been thrust from what was commonly considered a normal family life at an early age. Though rejected, he believed he was the one who had rejected conventional families with their working-class values and attitudes and their normal, boring lives, as well as the hypocrisy accompanying that way of life.

Dwayne was also very tough; he had endurance, and an incredible inner strength. Perhaps this was something he'd acquired from being on his own since his early teens. If his friends were doing something he wasn't into, he said he was the type to leave, or simply say it wasn't his scene, even though he belonged to the bikers.

That individuality, he explained, was something that was reinforced by Bob and Bonnie Colquhoun, whom he boarded with as a teenager in the early 1970s, for $100 a month. They were like a mother and father to him, two persons who had finally taken a keen interest in him but who were liberal enough to let him just be himself.

Dwayne had no time for liars, but could tolerate the

odd bullshitter; his motorcycle friends related fish tales about how they had told off the police when they were hassled for riding their Harleys. Dwayne, too, was known to exaggerate, brag, and talk tough. Townsfolk often heard that he'd boasted about carrying five Indian skulls on his belt, presumably meaning that he had killed five Natives. His bragging was likely his attempt to compensate for his height and lack of physical strength to win respect through fear and intimidation. He was only five foot six, and his friends referred to him as a "short shit."

Another tall tale in The Pas related how Dwayne had thrown Natives off the Bignell Bridge into the Saskatchewan River. Not only Dwayne, but also The Pas Bikers purposely spread this misinformation to try to frighten off the Indians – the enemy at that time – to warn them just how tough the bikers were.

Another tale, which many townsfolk claim to be true, was that the Natives were irritated by Dwayne's loudmouthed tactics and wanted to teach him a lesson. They placed Dwayne on the railings over the bridge, as he screamed and dangled in mid-air for help. The RCMP reportedly were the ones who had to rescue him.

Dwayne could be generous to a fault if he felt that person was good and sincere; he could feel sympathy towards someone who was hard done by. That's probably because he wasn't handed a hefty lot in life. For whatever reason, he didn't get along with his mother that well in his teenage years. Friends say he referred to his mother as "the hooker," presumably because she was seen frequently in bars with other men, something he couldn't understand. To Dwayne, a woman should always stick by her man, no matter what the problem. It's simply her place.

Another trait that really stands out about Dwayne is his street smarts. He also had his own sense of right and wrong, which included not "squealing" or "ratting" on people. No matter what, he would not speak to police. It's something most bikers just wouldn't and still don't do.

Both bikers and cops have their rulebooks about what is right and wrong. For cops it is Canadian law, a real book called the Criminal Code. For bikers, it is the Biker Code of Ethics, a list of made-up rules that just about every biker learns when he gets his Harley. The rules are simple enough: you don't talk to cops, whether they harass, beat, or threaten you. Never squeal or rat and never let a cop see you rattled.

To many bikers, cops are corrupt. They represent the hypocrisy of law and order, the glory-seekers. They buy and do dope but arrest others for trafficking and possession. They drink heavily and drive but charge others with impaired driving. They talk tough, but will go three on one to get what they want. They will trick, lie, cheat, and steal to get information. To bikers, cops are scheming, power-tripping men, most of whom are stupid flatfoots. Bikers probably make these judgments of police after hearing the odd story about the bad cop, and, like those fish tales, it gets embellished and exaggerated.

Police, of course, don't have much of a penchant for bikers, either, mostly because some of them are involved in heavy drugs and crimes. And if they aren't, they usually know who is. They are considered by some police to be the scum of society – the maggots running for cover when you turn over a rock. They make every cop's job hard because they don't talk, no matter how pleasant or how approachable a cop is. In any event, both sides hold equally strong stereotypes of each other.

There are police who say Dwayne, in his youth, was a greasy, long-haired troublemaker. Confrontational, extremely obnoxious, and mouthy, he rebelled against everything, and was a legend in his own mind. He and his friends who rode around town would poke fun at cops and had nicknames for all of them, including ''Good Night'' for Constable Donald Knight because they thought he was sleepy and off the mark. They got into scrapes just about every night of the week, and they rode loud, noisy bikes with choppers, similarly to the ones in *Easy*

Rider. Even Dwayne was known to get into fights, many of them with Natives. And most of the time he didn't win, mostly because he was much smaller than the rest of his gang.

"I'd see him in the Gateway and there'd be this little lump in a black leather jacket buried underneath some Indian," one friend recalled. "He'd defend himself but he wasn't that good of a fighter."

He also wasn't much of a friend of Lee Colgan, Jim Houghton, or Norm Manger – they weren't the types of men he wanted to be seen with. Lee and Jim were what Dwayne referred to as the upper crust of society, rich folk, even though economically they straddled the working and middle classes.

But Lee and Jim, as many people thought, were born with all the gifts of a perfect family and had no reason to project themselves as anything else. And Norm Manger was more of a hanger-on. Be it a party or a bar, Norm, a timid, introverted man, would be there.

But Dwayne hung around with some very judgmental bikers and had to protect his reputation as a tough guy – hanging around with a weakling and nice smiling guy just didn't fit the bill. As well, Dwayne didn't approve of Lee and Jim, mostly because he said they "did" Native girls, something bikers considered wrong or uncool. As he put it, "They weren't my people." It's not that Dwayne hated Native girls, it's just that they were as foreign to him as those people who knew nothing about Harley-Davidsons.

CHAPTER FOUR

It was bitterly cold and dark just after suppertime when Lee Colgan managed to borrow his dad's white '67 Chrysler for the night. It was November 12, 1971.

Colgan was cruising around The Pas, as usual looking for girls to party with, when he pulled up in front of the Cambrian Hotel. There he met up with Dwayne Johnston, Norman Manger, and his good buddy, Jim Houghton. Johnston didn't normally chum around with the three guys but for whatever reason he did that night.

The four drove around for several hours, drinking, laughing, chatting, telling the odd crude joke, and making quite a few trips to the vendor before Colgan asked his buddy, Jim Houghton, to take over the wheel at about midnight because he was too smashed to drive.

The four men were all very drunk by this time but that didn't matter. They ran out of booze and wanted more, so Houghton drove over to the Mallard Apartments on Seventh Street. Colgan and Houghton got out of the car and broke into the apartment of their buddy, Jack Halliday, and took two bottles of Red Devil wine, the extra-strength stuff they knew would do the trick in no time.

Some time during the night – he can't remember when – Brian Johnson and a friend hitched a ride with Manger and Houghton, but Lee Colgan's driving was so bad and the car was fish-tailing so much that Johnson got out. Johnson continued walking down Bignell Avenue when the white Chrysler pulled up beside him again. This time, Houghton was driving. They picked up Johnson again and let him out later that night.

The only version we have of the killing consists of the drunken recollections of two men, Lee Colgan and Norm Manger, who testified sixteen years later on the witness stand that they'd left Betty Osborne for dead in the bush.

In court, Colgan said that he, Houghton, Johnston, and Manger had just opened the bottles of Red Devil wine and taken a few swigs when they noticed an Indian girl walking west along a dimly lit Third Street. "Hey, do you want to go to a party?" they had asked her. The girl, Betty Osborne, had said no.

Colgan also testified that Dwayne Johnston, sitting in the back seat of the passenger side of the car, had rolled down the window and began chatting to Betty as they slowly cruised by. He invited her to go partying but, "She said she didn't want to go," Colgan said.

We do not know – nor will we ever – if Betty noticed Lee Colgan, the one man in the car she would have known. What we do know is that Colgan told the court that the car had stopped and Manger opened the front door of the two-door Chrysler. Then, Colgan said, Johnston climbed out of the back seat to try to convince Betty Osborne, a complete stranger, to get in. When she refused, Johnston pulled her into the middle of the back seat, shoving her between Colgan and himself. Betty resisted but the four men were determined to convince her to have sex with them all.

On a cold dark night, they drove Betty north on icy Highway 10 for about twenty miles, Colgan said. Laughing and drunk, the four men called each other such names as Frank, Dave, Joe, or Sam as they were pawing at her, forcing her to drink, and telling her they wanted her to screw all four. However, Betty Osborne might well have recognized Lee Colgan from Cornelius's basketball team. Colgan said they called each other by different names "so when we brought her back to town she wouldn't be able to say who she was with."

The four men kept asking Betty if she wanted some Red Devil wine and pushed the bottle under her lips and against her face. She said no in her thick Cree accent, and pushed the bottle away with her hands, Colgan told the jury.

That's when Johnston began arguing with Betty and tried forcing her to down the wine. When Betty started pushing back, Johnston pulled at her blouse and tore it, exposing part of her breast. The three other men laughed, chatted, and continued passing the bottle around.

Johnston kept fighting with Betty and she with him. When it looked as if she was giving back as much as she was getting, Colgan grabbed her arms and pinned them down by her sides. At the preliminary hearing Colgan testified that he was trying to protect Johnston because he thought she would scratch his eyes out. Once she was trapped, Johnston repeatedly grabbed at her while she cried out for help.

As Betty was repeatedly being smacked and punched and as she screamed for help, Houghton and Manger passed the bottle around as if nothing was happening. Houghton didn't pull the car over. He did nothing but assist these men into taking her to a secluded, desolate spot.

As Betty broke free from Colgan's hold, she started swinging her arms at Johnston, trying to fend him off. That's when Colgan cupped his hand over her breast and massaged it. "I thought it might be a little fun to see if I could get my hand onto her breast, too," he said.

Johnston meanwhile continued to argue and push her. Colgan said Houghton and Manger kept drinking while the woman was being beaten and sexually assaulted in the back seat.

It was Houghton who drove the gang out to this parents' cabin, apparently hoping she would "do" all four guys. The car rolled down to a snow-covered cabin at the end of a dead-end road and Betty Osborne was dragged out of the car by Johnston on a pitch-black night. The other three got out of the car, passing the bottle around and watching the late-night entertainment – Betty Osborne being beaten and stripped by Johnston. Colgan said he wasn't positive but that he thought Betty's bra was ripped off as he stood nearby watching.

Betty's screams were so shrill and loud that the men were afraid she would wake the neighbours. They decided to take her somewhere else. Colgan helped Johnston push the hysterical young woman onto the back seat of the car. Colgan said he assisted her because he thought it wouldn't be nice to leave her alone at the cabin.

It was at this point, Colgan said, that the four drove the beaten, bleeding girl a mile and a half to the secluded pumphouse area to calm her down. Houghton parked the car right in front of the pumphouse on the snowy lake side.

As the snow crunched under the tires, Betty and Johnston swung at each other while she screamed continuously for help. At the pumphouse there were no lights or people, just the sound of the biting wind.

Johnston then dragged Osborne out of the car while the other three men stayed in the warmth. "We were passing the bottle back and forth, listening to the radio, and we could hear some banging going on against the side of the car or the back of the car . . . I thought she was getting beat up," Colgan stated.

Colgan then asked Houghton, a bigger man, to get out of the car and help Betty, thinking he was the only one who would be able to handle Johnston. Colgan said he was too afraid of Johnston to help the girl, even though Johnston was small and outnumbered. As Houghton opened the door to get out, the inside roof light went on and Colgan caught a quick glimpse of Betty. She was upright but she hardly had any clothes left on.

From that moment on Colgan didn't hear a sound until

Diagram 1
Osborne   N.° 26421

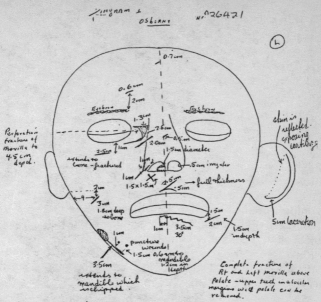

Perforation fracture of maxilla to 4.5 cm depth.

chin is reflected exposing cartilage

5 cm laceration

Complete fracture of Rt and Left maxilla above palate — upper teeth in a loosen margins with palate can be removed.

- bruising + scratching of Ⓡ face from eye level to chin — 5 cm x 10 cm.
- bruising + swelling of entire Ⓛ face from hairline to chin except for mid cheek area 3 cm x 4 cm.
- Buccal mucosa of upper lip contused + lacerated ē penetration to nostril — 4 cm x 3 cm.
- lower lip buccal mucosa lacerated in gutter to Ⓛ of midline over 4 cm in length ē irregular full depth penetration through skin wound
- complete fracture of nasal bone — multiple, ē adjacent multiple fractures of maxilla.

Pathologist's diagram indicating wounds to Betty Osborne's head and face

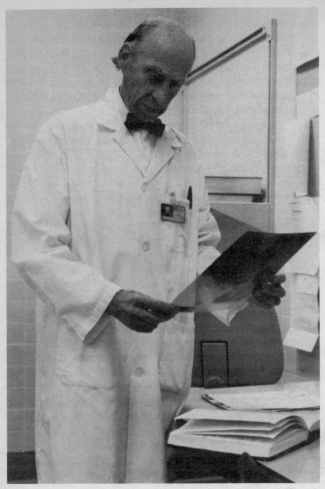
Pathologist Dr. Donald Penner (photo: Lisa Priest)

Johnston opened the driver's side of the door, reached under the seat, and pulled out a green-handled screwdriver. "What are you doing?" Colgan said he asked Johnston. Johnston didn't reply.

Colgan climbed into the front seat, and for the next minute or two he talked with Manger, trying to figure out what was going on outside.

Pathologist Dr. Donald Wills Penner said the killer or killers probably kneeled over Betty as they stabbed her naked body. He said they probably stabbed her repeatedly while she was lying nude on her back and then turned her over and smashed the screwdriver through her brain, back, ears – anywhere there was exposed flesh. "Anybody in a frenzy of wanting to kill someone keeps stabbing and beating frantically until the body stops moving," Penner said later.

Dr. Penner said about 49 of the 50 wounds on her body were likely made with the green-handled screwdriver tendered in court. He said it was only remotely possible the deepest wound – the one 5.5 centimetres deep into the head or 4.5 centimetres into the brain – was made with that screwdriver, leading the public to believe another screwdriver, perhaps the other one found on the road, may have been used as well.

Betty's naked body was dumped in the bush where it left a matted-down, bloodied imprint. It was then dragged by at least two men thirty-two feet and dumped in its final resting spot. Blood seeped from the holes in her body into the snow.

At least one of the men either jumped or stamped on Betty's face with a boot, causing blood to squirt two to three feet in every direction from the many holes in her head. It completely flattened her face so that she was unrecognizable.

Penner said he couldn't find any evidence of defence wounds, such as cuts or bruises to the hands, suggesting that Betty could have been unconscious when most of the stabbing took place. Another possibility is that one of the men held her while another carried out the beating and stabbing. He found no evidence of sexual intercourse.

"This wasn't an instanteous death for her," Dr. Penner said later. "It's terrible, awful when you see man's inhumanity to man. No matter how drunk you are, you know when you're hurting someone."

Colgan tried to figure out a plan of action. "I was talking to Norm for maybe another minute, just deciding what we should do and he said we should get out of there, so I started the car, pulled up back facing the road and stopped," Colgan said.

Shortly after he stopped the car, Colgan looked over at Manger. He was curled up into a ball under the dashboard of the car, whimpering.

Manger said he thought he was having a dreadful nightmare and when he looked around, he didn't think there was anyone else in the car with him. "I don't even know which window I looked out but it seemed like somebody was being dragged in the middle of no place," he said. "I remember that. And then I just said, 'Oh Christ,' 'cause I remembered that girl being in the car and I just thought that, God it seems so strange here and I just grabbed my head."

Colgan shone the headlights into the bush but couldn't see anything. Then he stopped, opened his window, and yelled for Johnston and Houghton, warning that if they didn't come he'd leave without them. "I looked at Norm," Colgan said. "I thought we were going to leave without them, and Norm was laying on the front floor of the car, curled up in a little ball and was crying." That's when Colgan yelled out one last time. I said, "If you don't come now we're leaving without you," and he heard one of the two men – he doesn't know which one – say, "Just a minute."

Houghton and Johnston came running from behind the car and jumped in the back seat. "I asked where she was and somebody from the back seat replied, 'She's dead,' so I started driving," Colgan said.

The murder would haunt Colgan for the next sixteen years. Never in that time would he have a decent night's sleep or be sober for more than a few months at a time.

Colgan drove the blood-splattered car from the remote area twenty miles down the icy, snowy highway back to town while someone in the back seat wiped the fingerprints from the screwdriver and threw it out the window, along with a blood-stained paper bag and pieces of Osborne's brassière. Colgan later said he may have asked one of them to get rid of the screwdriver.

It was then that the cabdriver driving along the road noticed what he thought was a piece of newspaper covered with red paint being thrown from a light-colored car when he passed it. He looked at the licence plate and remembered the numbers 42.

By this time it was 3:00 A.M., Colgan testified, and he and Jim decided to take in a dance at the Royal Canadian Legion Hall. They stayed for about half an hour. Colgan said he thought Johnston and Manger had been dropped off at the Cambrian Hotel.

It's not clear whether the men were trying to establish an alibi for the night or if they were so irrational they didn't consider whether anyone would notice a couple of guys in blood-splattered clothes.

Houghton pulled up at Colgan's house, parked the car and turned off the ignition. They discussed the killing for a few minutes and decided to keep it quiet. They agreed to see each other the next day, and Houghton got out of the car, walked across the street, and went home to sleep.

PART TWO

Life after Murder

CHAPTER FIVE

The pieces just didn't fit. The police had a badly mutilated body, pictures of blood-stained footprints, tire tracks in the snow, and a tattoo pledging a girl's love to Cornelius Bighetty. They had a cab driver's description of a car leaving the area of the murder scene early the previous morning and two numbers of a licence plate. They had found three pieces of the victim's torn, soiled clothing tucked under some rocks on the point, about 145 feet northwest of the pump house. But there was no motive, no suspects, and precious little physical evidence.

It appeared that Helen Betty Osborne had been sexually assaulted and died an extremely painful death. While the pathologist found no evidence of sexual intercourse, that didn't mean she hadn't been sexually assaulted. Grabbing and fondling would have constituted a sexual assault against Osborne – and it seemed a logical deduction that one had taken place, as her clothes had been ripped off.

Her killers were calculating, but not necessarily clever. They hid her white cardigan sweater, torn green denim pants, and purple, white and orange pullover, torn from the neck down, under some boulders, yet they left a trail of blood on the rocks. They dragged her deep into the bush, making it unlikely that anyone would find her, yet they left a path of blood-stained footprints. They left her high, shiny, black rubber boots on. They obviously hadn't been interested in her feet.

That Betty Osborne had fiercely fought off a sexual attack and lost her life doing it was clear; this fact would come out as evidence years later in court. This doesn't necessarily mean that she wouldn't have been killed had she complied; that's too simple. It's more likely the killers at one point realized they had gone too far and if Osborne lived to tell about it, they would be in big trouble, either with the police or certainly with those who loved her – a theory the prosecution would adopt at her murder trial sixteen years later.

But the real question revolved around how many had taken part in the beating and stabbing. It would take a lot of strength to stab someone fifty times. "After four or five times, you'd think the killer's arm would get tired," Chief Investigator Don Knight remarked. "Especially with a blunt weapon."

One thing the police definitely knew was that at least two individuals had been involved in bringing her to the place of her death. There were two sets of footprints on either side of the area where Osborne was dragged and then left for dead. Five tracks led to the murder scene and five tracks led out. Police noted three distinct sets of footprints among the tracks, meaning as many as three persons could have been involved. But so far, police had nothing to go on except some physical evidence, gut instinct, and training.

Basic training tells every cop that proving motive is one of the most important facets of a murder investigation. And more often than not, killers know their victims. The more passionate the killing, the stronger the connection usually is. It's not often a total stranger is picked up, killed so fiercely, and then dumped. But Knight couldn't even eliminate strangers. The question he kept mulling over and over was who could be capable of such brutality.

The picture of Osborne's nude, mutilated body was something Knight couldn't forget, but he couldn't afford to dwell on it, either. It was Sunday, November 14, the beginning of what was to be a very long, tiring day, looking for more evidence, interviewing more towns-people, and tracing and retracing the killers' steps. There weren't even enough pieces to put half the puzzle together and the pressure to get more evidence was on.

Knight and a few other officers drove back out to Clearwater Lake on that very cold Sunday morning. With Knight was Vance Menhennit, a dog master with two years' experience, who always travelled with a 110-pound German shepherd called Buck. The dog got its name after it was sold to the RCMP for one dollar from a kennel. Apparently, Buck was a little too big and fierce to carve out a career as a show dog, but he quickly landed a full-time job with the police, usually sniffing for human scent or scaring off rowdies at the Gateway Hotel on weekend nights.

Buck had been particularly helpful the day before, sniffing out Osborne's torn, bloodied clothing 145 feet northwest of the pumphouse. Menhennit knew he would be walking around across miles and miles of tarmac with the giant dog today, looking for a murder weapon and any more clothing or clues he might find. And Knight would be in his cruiser alongside, ready to take notes and file reports of any evidence they might find.

Menhennit decided to take Buck down along the pro-vincial Highway 287, the trunk route leading to the airport and pumphouse. He walked up and down the two-lane highway as Buck sniffed the ice-covered road, the shoul-der, and the ditches full of snow on both sides.

Around 1:45 P.M., three quarters of a mile from the murder scene, Buck began to run, pulling Menhennit down the road. There they found a small pair of bloodied, blue gloves, two pieces of a white, cotton bra with splat-ters of blood on it, and a blood-stained paper bag.

Those items were about a half-mile from the airport turnoff. Three weeks later, on December 6, a young man named Ron Garth Jones would be vigorously interrogated by police about the evidence. He had apparently spotted the items near the airport on the weekend of the murder while hitchiking towards town and told a local guy about it in a bar. Jones told police he couldn't remember if he had tampered with the articles but, in any event, he turned out to be a false lead.

Buck started sniffing his way back along the highway. Around three o'clock, about one and a quarter miles from the pumphouse, Buck pushed his nose onto the shoulder and yanked Menhennit down into the ditch. Lying in the snow was a green-handled screwdriver splashed with blood. Police took a picture of the blood-drenched screwdriver and then picked it up with gloves, being careful not to disturb any fingerprints. The screwdriver had interchangeable ends stored in its hollow handle but the one on the end of the shaft was small, thin, and flat-lathed. Drops of blood covered the shaft, leading Knight to believe that this screwdriver could have made the deep puncture wound near Osborne's nose and right eye. This was almost certainly a murder weapon if not the murder weapon.

They kept going, knowing there might well be more evidence. While Buck was sniffing, Menhennit kept his eyes peeled for anything that might strike him as odd or out of place. He would have to look at any disturbances in the snow, just in case the killer had buried any evidence. But this homicide was beginning to look like the act of a frantic, frenzied killer who'd panicked – someone who hadn't even thought to hide the victim or the murder weapon.

Several days later a middle-aged man named Russell Embury went to the RCMP with a flat-lathed screwdriver he had found lying on the highway the afternoon following the murder. An airport employee, Embury thought he'd better take it to the police after hearing that a young Native woman had been found stabbed to death. Unfortunately, the screwdriver had been sitting in a pail in the back of Embury's truck for several days and there was no blood or fingerprints on it.

Menhennit spent the better part of the day fruitlessly looking for more evidence. He continued to look for clues and any leads almost every day for the next month and a half, but found nothing. All Buck found was a new place to run in the wilderness.

Back at the office that same Sunday, Knight ate dinner while typing up stacks of reports. Every item they found had to be described in detail, identified by place and time, and then bagged and stored away. Volumes of reports, interviews, and statements had to be filed, read, and re-read first by his superiors and then by their superiors to make sure everything was in order should the case ever go to court.

The few pieces of physical evidence didn't give them much to go on. Perhaps the strongest lead was the two numbers on a licence plate. Trying to pin that to a car was another matter, however. These numbers were run through a computer to check against thousands of combinations of licence-plate numbers along with owners' addresses and vehicle registrations. Police then had to check out each file and politely ask people if they might search their cars.

Two days later, the Mounties, during their door-to-door interviews, asked Lee Colgan if he knew anything about the killing. Colgan subsequently testified that he hadn't told anything to the police but did inform his father about his involvement in the killing; the elder Colgan then took him to see a lawyer in town. Over the next few days, the police continued their interviews.

Meanwhile other officers were questioning Cornelius Bighetty. He became a murder suspect after an officer saw his name tattooed on the victim's leg and the tattooed initials C.B. on the base of her left thumb near her wrist. Perhaps he also became a suspect because this murder reeked of passion and uncontrolled fury. Murder victims have almost always of the same race as the killers, according to Dr. Donald Penner. "That's why I thought the Betty Osborne murder was so unusual," Penner said later. "Native people usually kill their own and whites usually only killed whites."

Cornelius later said kids were picked up from Margaret Barbour Collegiate and the Guy Hill residential school in droves, driven to the police station, interrogated, and in some instances put in jail. He was devastated when he heard that Betty – the woman he loved – had been killed. Seventeen years later he still called her one of the greatest loves of his life, a woman he would have married when he matured. But the day after the murder, hard reality had set in. Betty was dead. Cornelius was now a suspect.

In the interrogation room, two police officers tried using the technique of "good cop, bad cop" on him. This technique is often shown on TV police shows but is now considered old-fashioned. One officer vigorously interrogates the suspect. He plays the part of an impossible cop who won't listen to any answers, who degrades and dehumanizes the victim, trying to rattle him as best he can. He's hard, tough, and extremely irritable. No amount of reasoning or friendliness can jolt him. But just when his treatment begins to work on the suspect, the "good" cop tells him to give the person a break. He tries to cool down the hot-headed, "bad" cop. The suspect is relieved, lets down his guard a bit: That's when the "good" cop zooms in. He speaks in a friendly manner to the suspect, pretends he's on his or her side, and explains very logically and rationally what the other cop "really" wants from him, which is, of course, the truth. At that point, the suspect is supposed to crack or at least to soften.

But Cornelius wouldn't crack. He wouldn't say anything. "They kept saying: 'We know you're the one who did it,' and I said nothing," he recalled. Finally, Cornelius told them he didn't kill Betty. "I told them she was my girlfriend but they didn't seem to believe I didn't do it."

At one point in the interrogation, Cornelius said he

was shown gruesome colour photographs of Betty's mangled nude body taken at the murder scene. The photographs were stuck inches away from his face and shuffled like flashcards; each one showed a bloodied body from a different angle. "Then I went into shock and I passed out," he recalled. Someone waved smelling salts under his nose and then he woke up.

But Cornelius still wasn't very co-operative, mostly, he says, because he was so frightened. After the interrogation he was thrown in jail for a couple of hours. "They figured I must have something to hide but I wasn't used to this and I didn't want to talk about it."

Those two hours gave Cornelius time to think, and he agreed to take a polygraph test. Some of the questions he was asked were simple enough. Where had he been the night of the killing? When was the last time he'd seen Betty? What was their relationship? Did he have a clue who could have done this to her? After the lie detector test, Cornelius was quickly eliminated as a suspect. Other Indian kids started taking the same test and they were let go as well.

But the interrogations continued; the stubborn police would not give up. There were times when they were incredibly frustrated because they had a hunch that people knew more than they were telling. They began looking at men with criminal records and in the bush camps. They randomly pulled over cars, looking for licence plates with the numbers 42 on them. They continued to make door-to-door inquiries, desperately trying to find anyone who knew anything about the killing, each time wondering if the killer would be behind the next door. Police also went to the infamous Nip House, an all-night hangout where barflys congregated after the pubs closed and where most of the blackmarket trading took place. It's also a favourite place for plotting and rehashing crimes. That gave them a few leads, but nothing substantial.

Four days after the murder, on Wednesday, November 17, Betty Osborne's murder made front-page news in

The Pas Herald, a bi-weekly paper. The headline read: "Police Seek Clues Into Girl's Death." Below the head- line was a single-column picture of Betty wearing black- rimmed glasses and this brief story:

> The body of Miss Betty Osborne, 19 years, whose picture appears above, was found in the bush by a local youth while hunting rabbits near the Clearwater Lake Airport, northeast, The Pas, Manitoba, at approxi- mately noon last Saturday, November 13.
>
> RCMPolice, The Pas Rural Detachment advise that the deceased was apparently driven from The Pas to the vicinity of the airport, sometime after 12 o'clock midnight Friday night where she was viciously beaten and then dragged into the bush to die.

The story also included a public appeal, asking anyone who had information to call the police.

Few did. Some people would politely say they knew nothing when police asked them. Others bordered on the belligerent. Some townspeople were mysteriously eva- sive; others rambled on about gossip they had heard. There were rumours that someone from CFI had done it or that a crazed psychopath had driven into town and was ready to kill any Native girl he could get his hands on. And then there were rumours that three local young men had done it. As horrifying a thought as it was, at least that made more sense than the other rumours. But police were still bumping into false leads. The townspeople, now familiar with gossip that Lee Colgan, Jim Houghton, Dwayne Johnston, and Norm Manger had been involved, were tight-lipped with the Mounties.

CHAPTER SIX

Even though the four young men agreed to keep the killing quiet, Lee Colgan just couldn't shut up. And the first person he confessed it to was his father, who took him straight up town to see lawyer D'Arcy Bancroft.

It was just days after the killing. Bancroft told Lee's father to sit in the waiting room until the pair had finished talking. Bancroft welcomed Lee into his office and told him to make himself comfortable, directing him to a plush chair opposite his desk, right next to his mynah bird. Then Lee began unravelling the details of that very horrible night while Bancroft tried to keep up with his notes.

Lee rambled on about the night of the killing, about how intoxicated he and the others had been. He gradually became more nervous, every so often glancing, irritated, at the squawking mynah bird hanging over his shoulder. Bancroft's bird was unique: it defecated without warning at a forty-five degree angle in any direction. And it wasn't selective – it crapped on Bancroft's law partners, Crown attorneys, and even Queen's Bench judges.

After Lee finished his story, Bancroft instructed him to say nothing to anyone about the killing. "Bancroft said he knew everything about it already and that we'd just keep it quiet," Colgan said later in court. Bancroft had told him that all the cops had was circumstantial evidence. Lee's best bet was to exercise his legal rights and not talk to the cops, or to anyone else. And Bancroft was right. There were no fingerprints on the blood-drenched screwdriver, no eyewitnesses, and as long as the four men kept quiet, police would never be able to get a murder conviction. Lee had been even smart enough the morning after the killing to clean off the splatters of blood from the back fender of his father's car with a damp rag. All the cops had were two digits of a licence plate number. Lee promised to take the advice and maintain a pact of silence. But it was a promise Lee would break often.

When Bancroft told Colgan he already knew everything about the killing, he might have been relying on gossip he'd picked up; more likely, he'd learned the details from Dwayne Johnston. Johnston had approached his friend and lawyer, Bancroft, in his home shortly after the killing to tell him what happened. "He said: 'Don't tell me here,' and so we went for a drive in his car and he told me to not worry about it, that they didn't have anything on me," Johnston said in an interview afterwards.

The young, upstart lawyer – he was twenty-seven at the time – also saw Jim Houghton and Norm Manger. It's not clear if he saw Houghton, Manger, and Colgan together or separately after the murder; but Bancroft gave them all the same advice: keep a lid on the killing. Representing all four men was an extremely unusual burden for a lawyer to carry, but a legal one.

We do not know – nor will we ever know – if the four men told Bancroft exactly what happened the night of the killing. But one thing is certain. In 1971, a person could be charged with non-capital murder even if he was at the scene of the killing. All four men could have been charged for murder had they confessed to police, as Bancroft likely would have told them.

By now, news of Betty Osborne's death had spread like a prairie fire. Parents from northern reserves yanked their kids from the desegregation program at Margaret Barbour Collegiate and brought them back home. Betty's roommate, Muriel Robinson, packed her bags shortly after the murder and left for her Cross Lake home. She told Mrs. Benson she was too distraught to carry on her schooling and that she didn't feel safe in The Pas any more. Native girls who stayed in school were warned by their parents and landlords to walk in pairs and never to go out at night.

Meanwhile, at Norway House, Justine Osborne celebrated the birth of her new baby, Andrew, by Jimmy Osborne, and mourned her eldest child's death, unable to come to grips with why anyone would hurt her daughter.

Betty's sister, Cecilia, nine years her junior, vividly remembers the open-casket funeral. As family and friends lined up to kiss Betty in her coffin, Cecilia stayed behind. "I was scared to get close to her," she recalled. "She looked very different. Her face was all messed up." Before the casket was about to be removed, however, Cecilia had a change of heart. She leaned over the coffin and noticed the caked-on makeup, a mortician's attempt to mask the savage stabbing. She kissed Betty, who had dressed her for school and taught her how to colour. "I'll never forget the smell of that make-up powder," she said. "Every time I smell makeup, it brings it all back."

The family couldn't afford a tombstone so Justine asked a man on the reserve to build a wooden cross. The cross and a bunch of fresh-cut flowers were placed on Betty's grave.

Justine's second eldest child, seventeen-year-old Isaiah, couldn't make it for the funeral. Weeks earlier he had been taken from his home in Norway House and put in a foster home because of his lengthy record of thefts. Justine had experienced several devastating losses that month and it must have been one of the most trying times of her life. Cornelius was too upset to go to the funeral. (He still played sports with his classmate Lee Colgan, oblivious to Lee's involvement in the killing of his former love.)

After Betty Osborne's death made the headlines in *The Pas Herald*, it was quickly dropped. There were no follow-up stories, no letters to the editor, and no editorials. It would be another fourteen years before Betty Osborne's death made the headlines again and another two before her killers' trial caught the attention of the national media.

Lee Colgan continued going to school, working and cruising for girls on weekends with Jim Houghton. Two weeks after the killing, Lee ushered guests at his brother Rick's wedding at the Ukrainian Catholic Church in The Pas. Meanwhile, Dwayne Johnston kept hanging around his biker friends and Norm Manger got more wasted on booze, burrowing himself into a netherworld of drunkenness and street living.

The following weekend Lee and a few other guys got some beer from the vendor and went to a party in an abandoned house in The Pas. It wasn't often teenagers were able to find abandoned houses, and when they did they really partied; they knew they could trash the place.

Lee was drinking quite heavily as usual, and managed to get a woman to sit in a car with him and listen as he poured out his troubles. (According to a bail hearing transcript, the woman said she had worked in The Pas as a waitress and stopped in town with a friend to pick up her things before moving back home to Saskatchewan. She was never identified or found by police.) Whether prompted by an act of conscience or the desire to impress the woman, Lee told her how "they" had killed an Indian girl by stabbing her with a screwdriver the previous weekend, and he mentioned at least two other men.

Naturally, it must have been horrifying for her to be trapped in a car on a pitch-black night while a man she knew only by sight described the brutal murder of that Native girl she'd heard about. She made the mistake of telling her boyfriend, a friend of Lee's, what she had heard, and he warned her to keep her mouth shut, or else. Unfortunately, this threat had a lasting impact on her and it would be another six months before her conscience caught up with her. While visiting her brother in Michigan, she coaxed him into writing an anonymous letter to the police in The Pas, telling them everything Lee had told her and when.

Lee told more and more people about the killing after that – people in bars, stores, and even people at work. He continued to work at Fishman's for a few more months, until he finished paying off the $900 debt sometime later in 1972.

One week after the murder, Lee told several employees at a downtown store about the killing. They had been standing around the check-out counter discussing how they had seen a dozen cops buzzing around the pump-house. As the employees continued to speculate about who killed Betty Osborne, Lee dropped a bombshell. He said that he, Norm Manger, Dwayne Johnston and Jim Houghton had picked up the girl and yanked her into the car. He quite matter-of-factly told his audience of three dumbstruck store employees that they had told the Native girl they wanted to have sex with her. Lee said the girl, distraught and angry, swore in her thick Cree accent that, "No white man will ever have sex with me." And she was told, "If you don't, we're going to kill you."

As the employees stood gaping in amazement, Lee continued to unravel his story, almost as though spinning some folksy yarn. He said that he and the guys had driven her out to Houghton's cabin, hoping she would "put out," but she had resisted fiercely. They had taken her to another location where they had "finished her."

The workers, in their teens at the time, said they didn't go to police with Lee's story because it was only hearsay evidence. They figured if they knew about it, the police most certainly would as well. This line of thinking would eventually be adopted by the entire town.

The gossip about the four local boys' involvement was spreading like wildfire in The Pas. Within a few weeks, Lee said later, just about everyone in town knew who was involved in the killing of Betty Osborne. That's mostly because he was telling everyone. Some accounts, oddly enough, didn't include Dwayne Johnston. Others did. "It was getting so bad that he was telling people the same story twice," a friend recalled. "There wasn't a person in town who didn't know what was going on."

Unfortunately these rumours didn't seem to be getting back to the police. As Mounties went door to door, townspeople became evasive. Even though Colgan's friends and many others had heard his confessions, they said nothing to police. "He told me he was there and he knows what happened and asked me what I think he should do about it and I told him, 'You should go to the police,' said Steve Maksymetz, a businessman in The Pas. "I just didn't think it was my responsibility – it's up to the police to handle something like that." Others whom the police questioned said they knew nothing even though they did; they just didn't want to get involved. As for those who never went to police, many of them figured Lee would deny his involvement anyway, so what good would it do. Some of them rationalized it: the murder was done and over with, so why belabour it.

Just about everyone in town heard rumours about the killing and about all four names connected to it. If they didn't pick up the information from Lee, they got it at the pool hall, The Royal Canadian Legion, the barber shop, just about anywhere people talked. "Within a week or two weeks after it happened it was quite common knowledge around town that the four of us were involved," Colgan said later in court. Gossip was rife in the town and it was quickly becoming a parlour topic, with each townsperson speculating on which of the four local boys had driven the screwdriver through Betty Osborne's body.

The murder was embellished hundreds of times over, each version adding another gory detail about the victim's injuries. Townspeople would talk with great knowledge about how Betty Osborne's eyes were gouged out with a screwdriver, how she was repeatedly gang-raped by the boys after she was killed and how she died just to save

her virginity, when all she really had to do was comply
– as if there were measures she could have taken to save
her own life, but out of stupidity or sheer foolishness,
she decided to die. And that line of thinking cast much
of the guilt from the young men; townspeople heard she
had been given fair warning that she should consent to
having sex with the four or die; it should have been a
simple enough choice, especially for an Indian girl.

The rumours, however, didn't stop townspeople from
talking to the boys and their parents or inviting them out
to parties, dinners, and Sunday barbecues; they just never
mentioned that very unfortunate evening. Some people
felt sorry for Lee's father, Bud. The poor man, they
thought. This murder is just ruining the Colgan family.

One reason for this silence was the portly Bancroft,
an intimidating figure who literally threw his weight around
town. He knew businesspeople in The Pas, was friendly
with crown attorneys, lawyers and judges, and was thought
of as part of the upper crust in town. He was known by
many lawyers for his eccentricities and intelligence, by
waitresses at the Gateway for his daily lunch of a steak
sandwich cooked blue rare, and by the tailors who cus-
tom-made his clothes; he was a good customer in The
Pas. And he was highly visible.

Of the dozen or so lawyers in The Pas, Bancroft was
considered to be a shining light at the firm Orchard,
Bancroft, Whidden, Mayer & Gardiner. Some called him
brilliant; others, overconfident, perhaps unjustifiably. At
times he seemed to be a young lawyer who'd become
enamoured of himself after winning a few cases, becoming insufferable to others because of his arrogance.
"D'Arcy was not a shrinking violet," said Bob Mayer,
his former law partner. "He knew he was good."

A native of Winnipeg, Bancroft was the only child of
a locomotive engineer. He articled with one of the province's top legal firms, Walsh and Micay, and was assigned to lawyer Greg Brodsky – the man who would

D'Arcy Bancroft with his pet ocelots (photo: Greg Brodsky)

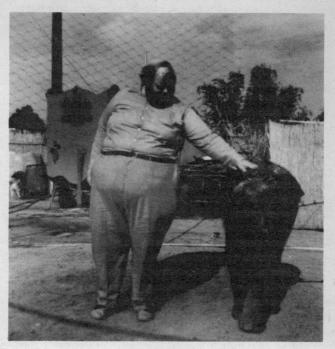

D'Arcy Bancroft

eventually act for one of his clients sixteen years later. After he finished articling, he moved up to The Pas and practised civil litigation and criminal law.

Bancroft had all of the trappings of success. Squeezed into his little two-seater sportscar, he would drive around The Pas and out to Flin Flon to watch his favourite football team, the Flin Flon Bombers. He even defended a couple of players. He also leased a luxurious Lincoln Continental Mark IV.

Bancroft was a fatalist. He predicted his own death before the age of thirty-five, after receiving a similar prognosis from his family physician. After having been warned to lose weight or die young, he occasionally managed to drop twenty or thirty pounds, but most people were hard pressed to see any change. "D'Arcy always said he planned to live like that for the time he was here," Mayer recalled.

Besides acting on various assault charges for young men in The Pas, Bancroft worked on the odd criminal case. Mayer recalled that his late partner had acted for a man who had hijacked an airplane with a sharpened toothbrush. In another case, he also managed to shut down a packing plant.

One of the things Bancroft's law partners did have difficulty with was his mynah bird. Bancroft, who had a strong love for wild animals, insisted on keeping it at his office, even though it would leave a thick paste of faeces on the wall. "And he would always come to work with his arms scratched after wrestling with his ocelots and leopards," Mayer recalled. "He really liked his wild animals."

Bancroft was an impatient man who detested bureaucracy. He boasted about being friends with Progressive Conservative Prime Minister John Diefenbaker. But no one really believed him. "We went to Ottawa back in 1967, just before the leadership campaign," Mayer recalled. "And then we went to Diefenbaker's office and I looked around and there's this note that says: 'D'Arcy

Bancroft called and the chief says, 'Come right in.' We were there talking with him for about an hour and a half.''

Despite Bancroft's idiosyncrasies, however, he earned the community's respect as an excellent lawyer, even when he represented all four men. Perhaps townspeople thought that if he was giving legal advice to the boys, they couldn't have been that bad. More likely, they feared repercussions from a man who had tremendous power and knew what circles to exercise it in.

And Bud Colgan, a heavy drinker himself, also knew how to exercise his influence. He too, was of good society, even though his favourite son was a drunk and drug user. Frank Houghton was a friendly meat-packing salesman with two lovely daughters, even though his son was a bit on the wild side. Dwayne Johnston hung around with Bancroft and had his confidence, his trust, and no one would interfere with that. Norm Manger was a nobody and his involvement didn't appear as great as that of the others.

Gossip of the murder spread among the Indian community on the north side of the Saskatchewan bridge as fast as it had in town. Indian men and women immediately labelled the four boys white scum; it didn't matter to them who smashed the screwdriver through Betty Osborne's skull because all four had been in the car that night but none of them had helped her. They felt her murder wasn't being investigated vigorously or thoroughly by police because she was Native – a squaw as most whites would say. Justine and the rest of the Osborne family had also heard rumours Betty was pregnant at the time of the killing.

There was nothing the Natives could do: they had no lobbying power, and weren't respected politically or socially and had no economic clout. They felt helpless and cheated, and their resentment and distrust of whites intensified. Many Indian girls who went to high school or hung out in bars memorized the faces of the four men, worried that they could be next. ''I was old enough to remember to stay away from those four guys,'' said Sandra De La Ronde, a Metis living in The Pas. Native and Metis girls felt unprotected by police, rejected by a white town, and defenceless against any white man who felt like yanking them off the street.

Like the townspeople, Natives speculated on ways the killing could have been prevented. Years later, evidence would show that, although she has been intoxicated, Betty Osborne clearly hadn't been interested in having a drink or sex with these men; if the four boys had truly wanted to calm her down, why didn't they just drop her off at a coffee house, apologize and smoothe things over? Even if Osborne had gone to police, would they have believed a drunken Indian girl, screaming hysterically in Cree?

Friction between the groups intensified. Natives felt townspeople weren't exercising their civic duty by telling police what they knew, it seemed, only because Betty Osborne was Native. The issue was not what evidence they could give or if it would have helped convict the killers. The point was that some people just didn't care enough to bother. As far as the Natives were concerned, the townspeople were acting in concert with the four boys and D'Arcy Bancroft, in a conspiracy of silence.

Police were frustrated by the lack of physical evidence. They had a body and a murder weapon. They didn't know who killed Osborne, even though most of the town did.

There had to be something that could break this case, the missing piece that would make the rest of the puzzle fit together. During each brainstorming session, the police would sit around a table with a big pot of coffee and lots of cigarettes, bouncing investigative techniques and tactics off one another for hours.

A few weeks after the killing Constable Thomas Boyle read Gerold Frank's *The Boston Strangler*. He was fascinated. In the book, the prime suspect, Albert DeSalvo, undergoes hypoanalysis, a combination of hypnosis and psychoanalysis, to recall women he had raped and strangled. That was it! Boyle made the seemingly outlandish proposal that they hypnotize cabdriver Phillip McGillivary to see whether he would remember the other numbers of the licence plate. Hypnosis was rarely used in police investigations back in 1971. In fact, it was considered bizarre, but anything was worth a shot.

On December 12, 1971 McGillivary strappped himself in a plane seat for the trip from The Pas to a small Saskatchewan town. Police told him there was nothing to worry about. He was to be hypnotized by a Roman Catholic priest from northern Saskatchewan. The officer assured him it wasn't black magic. The police emphasized to McGillivary that his help could have an integral part in helping solve this killing.

McGillivary, in his early fifties at the time, sat on the stiff leather divan and lay down. The priest who would be hypnotizing him pulled a thick gold medal on a chain from around his neck and began swinging it pendulum-like in front of the cabbie's face.

McGillivary was lulled into a deep sleep. The priest brought him back to November 13, 1971, between 3:00 and 4:00 A.M. McGillivary was driving his cab along the provincial truck route Highway 287, and passed a blue or light-colored vehicle driving back to town, about one-and-a-half miles from the murder scene. A piece of newspaper with what looked like red paint on it was thrown out of the car. Then the priest brought McGillivary to the licence plate. He had earlier reported to police that he saw two digits, numbers four and two. After a few minutes of probing, he murmured two other numbers, five and three. He believed the Manitoba licence plate number read 5342 but he couldn't remember the two letters before the numbers. Remembering the numbers in sequence was a gigantic help to police. Now all they needed was the car.

CHAPTER SEVEN

Don Knight leaned back in his chair, put his feet up on the desk and shuffled through the mail at The Pas rural detachment. Most of it looked dull from the outside – just bills, flyers, advertisements – and he tossed them aside. But one envelope with a U.S. stamp piqued his curiosity. Knight grabbed a nearby letter opener and slit the top of the envelope open.

Scrawled on a single sheet of paper was the description of a woman's conversation with Lee Colgan some six months earlier. The letter said she had been sitting in a car with Lee the weekend after the murder when he described the killing of a Native girl to her. Knight pulled the letter closer to his chest and frowned. Lee mentioned that two other men had been involved in the killing and that it had taken place in his dad's white Chrysler. The woman said she had been so alarmed that she coaxed her brother into writing this anonymous letter while she was vacationing in Michigan. She had been warned by her boyfriend to keep her mouth shut or else. So she had remained silent for six months. The letter landed on Knight's desk on May 5, 1972.

Knight read and reread the letter but he must have been skeptical. He must have wondered if the author of the anonymous letter was a mental case or if she was just trying to slander Lee. After all, why would it come so late, and why wouldn't she at least sign it or make a telephone call? But the car she described bore a licence plate whose numbers matched those the cabdriver had remembered under hypnosis. It seemed to fit.

It was the kind of break the police had been waiting for. While Knight said they knew two or three months after the killing that Colgan, Houghton, and Manger had been involved, they still didn't have enough evidence to take the three men to court. Knight said they even searched Houghton's room at his parents' home at 754 Constant Avenue in February 1972 – but it yielded nothing. By this time, it was a dead topic to townspeople in The Pas: the only time they mentioned it was when they speculated on why police weren't arresting anyone for it. It seemed obvious to them that the four men had killed her.

Townspeople began trickling into the police stations with what little information they had. But by this time, the hard information wasn't anything the cops didn't already know.

People went to police saying they'd seen so-and-so with blood on his shirt the other day and they thought he could have murdered Betty Osborne because his wife had died mysteriously and he'd probably done her in as well. But some townspeople had information that could have helped get a conviction early on because they heard Lee constantly confess to being involved in the murder. Many people who worked in bars and hotels or knew him from the street could have gone to police but didn't. Some even had a play-by-play description of the killing and knew who did it but never came forward.

But the police said an anonymous letter and four letters of a licence plate wouldn't be enough to get a warrant to search Bud Colgan's car. And they didn't ask permission from Colgan to search the vehicle because that would have given him a tip-off to clean the car and give it a more thorough going-over than he had done the morning after the killing. Instead, they said, they stepped up their inquiries around town and were rewarded when an informer of Knight's had told him in the spring of 1972 that a fourth man had been involved in the crime: Dwayne Johnston. They now knew the names of the four men who had ridden in the death car.

Then the police finally made their move. They drove to the cottage of provincial court Judge William R. Martin at Clearwater Lake to request his signature on a search warrant. Martin thought it odd that it had taken them so many months to ask, but he issued it and said nothing. The search warrant said that police believed there to be human blood, tools, and clothing inside a 1967 two-door white Chrysler Newport registered to a Mr. Harold Colgan. As well, they obtained warrants to look through the other men's homes for more evidence.

The following day, on June 20, 1972, an officer went to Bud Colgan's place of work, the Manitoba Liquor Control Commission, at 10:45 A.M. to seize the car. The officer showed Mr. Colgan the search warrant. Mr. Colgan briefly read the warrant and told him the car wasn't there; his wife, Joyce, had parked it in the parking lot of Keewatin Community College. Mr. Colgan said he'd telephone his wife to let her know the police were coming for the car.

The officer drove to the college, just off Seventh Street east. Mrs. Colgan was waiting at the front doors. When showed the search warrant, she handed over the keys, pointing through the window to the car – the one with licence plate BN 5342. The officer hopped into the driver's seat and drove it back to The Pas detachment where Don Knight and Corporal Harold Bielert were waiting to rip it apart.

Although it had been seven months since the killing, police were hopeful about finding something in the car that would provide enough evidence to take the case to court. But after all that time, the cops must have known the odds were slim. After all the car washes and interior vacuumings most cars go through in a few months, the most the cops could hope to find were a few hairs at best.

After all, if this was the car that had transported Betty Osborne to her death, surely the killers would have had the foresight to give it a thorough cleaning sometime during those seven months.

But Knight tackled the job with his usual fervour. He opened the door and took a quick glance at the back seat, immediately noticing a small stain. He took a closer look, quickly brushing his hand over the spot. It was a dark stain but it was too difficult to tell what it was or how long it had been there. He grabbed a pair of scissors, carefully cut around the seat, and put the swatch into a plastic bag. He noticed a similar stain on a small back-seat cushion and handed that over to Bielert as well. Knight didn't want to get his hopes up yet, but it appeared the stain was blood.

As well, he and Bielert grabbed a rear seat rest, fabric from the floor, and a tool kit. Both disassembled the interior and trunk of the car, looking under every nook and cranny for any piece of evidence they could find. What they had already found was one lucky break. But they couldn't believe their good fortune when Knight spotted a faded white brassière strap and metal clasp underneath the back seat. Even after seven months, a substantial amount of physical evidence had been left in the car. Why Lee Colgan never thought of cleaning it up remains a mystery.

Knight took the seat rest, stained fabric, bra strap, and clasp to the crime laboratory in Regina. Attempting to reconstruct the bra, a hair and fibre expert requested a Vogue brand, size 34A, style 122, for comparison. Police in The Pas hurriedly looked through the ladies' lingerie sections of department stores before finally finding a sample of the same brand and style, size 32AA, style 122. With that model, the expert reconstructed Betty Osborne's brassière with the strap, clasp, and two cups found near the murder scene. As well, they found 114 hairs on the rear seat rest and floor, eight of which had

The clothing Betty Osborne wore on the night of her murder
(evidence photo)

Bud Colgan's car (evidence photos)

similar characteristics to Osborne's. Police now had physical evidence showing that Betty Osborne had been in the car.

Once positive identification had been made with the blood type and, most importantly, the bra clasp, the Mounties went straight to Lee Colgan's house to get some answers. It's not known exactly how police put it to Lee, but they knew the circle was getting tighter. Betty Osborne had definitely been in the car at some point, and they knew it certainly hadn't been for any joy ride with Bud Colgan. It was time for Lee to confess.

When police told him what they had found in the car, Lee remarked in an arrogant, snotty tone: "Oh, the brassière and the blood – that doesn't prove anything," adding that he'd say nothing more because he was afraid of the other men involved in the killing, an excuse he would often repeat to friends and family. Police said there was nothing they could do because he wouldn't talk. And Lee knew it.

When the other three were questioned, they merely replied, "Go talk to D'Arcy." Norm Manger told police he hadn't been in the car that night, figuring it would be the perfect alibi. The cops didn't buy it.

It didn't take long before police decided to visit Bancroft's three-bedroom home on the south side of town. Posted on the outside of his home were two signs: Beware, Your Local Police Are Armed and Dangerous, and No Trepassing, Violators Will Be Eaten. As Bancroft opened the door, the officer stiffened. A waft of urine and faeces filtered through the screen door.

One of Bancroft's many eccentricities was that he loved letting wild animals roam freely in his home; some even had their own bedrooms. Bancroft had a leopard, two ocelots (Aristotle and one-eyed Lancelot), a chameleon, and two Siamese cats. All of them played together in harmony around the house – until the Siamese cats ate the chameleon, then were devoured by the ocelots.

In any case, D'Arcy Bancroft welcomed the officer

in. Everyone in town and even members of Winnipeg's legal community knew what it meant to be invited into Bancroft's home; they all had heard the stories. There was the infamous one about the Queen's Bench judge who was invited over to Bancroft's for tea: he had inadvertently awakened one of Bancroft's ocelots, which responded by tearing a huge chunk out of the seat of his lordship's trousers and gnawing on his buttocks. Then there's the one about the dog that constantly yapped at Bancroft's screen door. An irritated Bancroft let his leopard loose. It tore the dog apart, shutting him up for good. Still, there were things that many people liked and admired about Bancroft. Besides his quick mind, he had a very dry, almost morose sense of humour. For instance, he often feigned anger that airlines charged him for two seats, even though his huge form usually spread over three.

The officer asked whether Bancroft's clients could perhaps be a little more co-operative. After all, they were trying to solve a murder. The police must have known that having the suspects' hair samples would have been extremely helpful. They couldn't exactly go snipping hair off the heads of the four men – that would be in violation of their legal rights and therefore inadmissable as evidence in court. But no amount of sweet talk was going to soften Bancroft; he flatly stated that he wouldn't co-operate; the cop didn't have anything on the kids and if he were smart, he'd lay off.

Bancroft was a huge thorn in the side of the police. He was obnoxious, arrogant, at times belligerent and protected his clients with the same vigour as his leopard showed when it went after neighbourhood dogs. He often got his clients off and always did his homework. He was sharp, cocky, well prepared in court, and knew the ins and outs of the law. He knew he didn't have to assist the police, nor was there any legal reason to co-operate – that wouldn't have been in his clients' best interests.

But Bancroft went one step farther than the average

lawyer. He had a very strong paternal instinct and would often take his clients into his home, neglect to charge them for his services, lend them money, and help them out of any tight spots they had with police. He remained generous although he'd often been taken advantage of.

One of the clients Bancroft was sympathetic to was Dwayne Johnston. Years later, Johnston said he and Bancroft had been friends and used to discuss music, law, the cops in The Pas – just about anything of interest. The pair buddied around, went drinking together. To Johnston, Bancroft was a mentor who gave him specific instructions on handling cops. But even this advice wasn't enough. He constantly turned to Bancroft for help because one of the RCMP officers was pestering him. The officer often stopped Johnston on his motorcycle and told him that they knew he was responsible for the killing and it was only a matter of time before they nailed him for it.

Dwayne also told Bancroft the same officer had kicked him in the leg leaving a big, bloodied bulge. This occurred shortly after doctors had removed a cast treating a broken ankle. The harassment became so intense that Bancroft wrote a strident letter to Manitoba's attorney general and another to the RCMP. He even went to the chief investigator, Don Knight, whom he presumably hoped would act as a intermediary, saying the cops didn't have to harass his clients. Shortly after he wrote his letter the officer was transferred, although it's not known if that had anything to do with the harassment.

That summer, police pieced together a case with the little physical evidence they had and took it to the Crown attorney for approval. An extra piece of evidence came from a girl who had found a pair of black-rimmed glasses lying in a ditch near the pumphouse. One earpiece was missing. Engraved on them was the name Betty Osborne. After sending them to an optometrist and seizing Osborne's vision-testing records, police confirmed they had indeed belonged to the victim. But the blood stain on the back seat, brassière piece, glasses, and hair with similar characteristics to Betty Osborne's weren't enough: the Crown attorney told police the case wouldn't go beyond a preliminary hearing. Their best bet, he said, was to wait until the cops had enough evidence to make a conviction stick. Certainly, the blood, hair and fabric placed Betty Osborne in the car. What they couldn't prove, however, was that the four suspects had been there with her.

By this time, the case must have been getting ridiculously frustrating for police. It seemed as though they had about as much physical evidence as they could ever hope to find and the trail was getting cold. It was becoming a waiting game. Police knew Colgan was talking; it just wasn't to them. Those he did tell who came to the police had only hearsay evidence anyway, nothing the cops didn't already know but couldn't prove. Meanwhile, the Mounties kept on running into the four suspects on the street, in bars, and in restaurants.

It was the summer of 1972 when Constable Tom Boyle made the innocent mistake of going out for dinner at La Verendrye, a Chinese restaurant on the south side of town. Like most customers, he hung his jacket on the coat rack, forgetting his keys and other valuables in the pockets. Boyle noticed that one of the four suspects also happened to be dining there but didn't pay much attention to him. Boyle ate his dinner, had a couple of drinks, and was about to leave when he noticed his coat and keys were gone. So was the suspect. Paranoid that the four might have hatched some bizarre scheme to steal all the files on the case, he raced back to the detachment and called a locksmith to change the locks on the doors and filing cabinets at the two RCMP detachments situated within and outside of town. Such incidents made the police's job even more frustrating. Boyle never did get his keys back, but was always wary of what the suspect might do next.

Sixteen years later at a preliminary hearing, a man named Clint Scott Christiansen testified that he had driven out to Clearwater Lake with his friend Lee Colgan that same summer to check out a party when they spotted Dwayne Johnston walking along the road. The two had picked him up and drunk a couple of beers on the way to the lake. On the way back, Dwayne had asked to sit in the front seat but Clint had refused. Apparently, Dwayne had been so miffed by this that he'd pulled out a screwdriver from under the seat, stuck it under Clint's chin and said, "Do you want the same thing that fucking squaw got?" Clint told Lee to stop the car, dragged Dwayne out, and hit him a couple of times. Lee had to pull him off.

Clint's testimony at the preliminary hearing was rejected by defence lawyer John Scurfield, who suggested he had gone to police thirteen years after the incident only because an impaired driving charge against him had been dropped in exchange. The self-described alcoholic, who was put up in the Wescana Hotel and monitored by police to sober up for the hearing, was eventually dropped by the Crown and wasn't called to testify at the trial.

Since there was precious little physical evidence, the police must have known the only way to be sure of a conviction was to provoke a reaction from one of the four men. They knew Norm Manger was timid, constantly doped up, and wouldn't chat about the killing. Jim Houghton was just plain tight-lipped. Police felt Dwayne Johnston was doing everything in his power to intimidate the other men into not talking, even though he was seven years younger than Manger, five years younger than Houghton, and about fifty pounds lighter and several inches shorter than both.

Determined to provoke a confession, the police put them under surveillance. On street corners, outside bars, at their homes and jobs – you name it – the cops were there in unmarked cars looking conspicuously inconspicuous. In a small town where everyone knows everyone else, a car parked on a street corner gets noticed. The Mounties nevertheless would follow the four men, find out who they were hanging out with or where they were going, hoping to get some new leads. They did, but it was nothing substantial.

The four men were so fed up with the police following them that they told Bancroft, who decided to put an end to it by threatening to prosecute the police for conspiracy, watching and besetting, intimidation, and two counts of misusing licence plates. Bancroft apparently thought police had used the licence plates belonging to a town bus while sitting in their unmarked cars. In essence, Bancroft wanted to put a halt to their zealous investigation.

On September 26, 1972, Bancroft wrote two strident letters – one to the RCMP rural detachment, the other to Crown attorney T.M. Singh in nearby Flin Flon. On Orchard, Bancroft, Whidden, Mayer & Gardiner letterhead, Bancroft warned police that they were not above the law and shouldn't harass or assault his four clients. As well, he enclosed letters from Colgan, Houghton, Johnston, and Manger, which stated they didn't want to be questioned by the police. Bancroft's letter reads in part:

If you persist in accosting the above-named clients of the writer either at their residences, their jobs, on the street or at any other place it will be against their will and expressed wishes and there will be no doubt that you will be doing so wilfully and not out of ignorance.

Further, the above-named clients of the writer herewith demand that you cease to follow them. Your attention is drawn to the Privacy Act, a copy of which is enclosed. You will note the defence afforded to police and that your conduct could not conceivably fall within the protection of this defence. It would be difficult to show how you could obtain or hope to obtain evidence of an alleged offence 11 months after its purported commission by following people you suspect.

. . . The writers [sic] clients do not want to cause you trouble of any kind. They have no ax to grind against police. However, if their rights are violated they will do all things legally necessary to protect themselves. We would suggest you govern yourselves accordingly.

The letter to Crown Attorney T.M. Singh was similar, except for one very snide paragraph. Bancroft wanted to know why Singh questioned how he, Bancroft, could act for the four men, as if it was something out of the ordinary.

At any rate to put any doubts out of your mind the writer encloses photocopies of directions in writing to the R.C.M.P. signed by each of the four setting out the writer's authority and the wishes of the four about being questioned. These documents are clear in meaning and copies will be sent to various members of the R.C.M.P. As well, he accused police of harassing seven people, including himself and his four clients.

In the past you advised the writer that you have advised the police that when any person says they don't want to talk to them the police should not continue to ask questions. You said that in the event that questioning persisted you advised the police any statements acquired would not be tendered. And that in fact you would not tender them in court.

The writer knows you be a man of your word. The writer knows police do not do work for nothing. He therefore expects no more attempts to ask questions to his clients aforesaid.

The writer, on behalf of his clients, is of the opinion the R.C.M.P. involved have commited the following criminal or quari-criminal offences:
  (1) Conspiracy
  (2) Watching and besetting
  (3) intimidation
  (4) mis-use of licence plates (two counts)
And then it ends with this paragraph:

You have the means of ascertaining the identity of

these [police] involved. We trust you will ensure that these violations are punished. The writer will collect what further evidence you require on request and furnish copies of signed statements [from his clients].

Police immediately thought the letters threatening. But that wasn't going to stop them from investigating the murder. The cops continued to question Dwayne Johnston. Boyle recalled that they had hinted to him that they hadn't forgotten about the killing. Once, at the police station, "We said, 'There's something missing here, Dwayne; where's your screwdriver?'" Boyle recalled. "We had him shaking pretty good."

After the murder, Lee Colgan began drinking more and more, and continued to talk about the killing, trying to conquer the nightmare. Police would have loved it had he shot his mouth off in their hearing – they desperately wanted a confession from him. They tried provoking him a number of ways but there was one tactic they were particularly notorious for. They'd wait for Lee to enter the Royal Canadian Legion, the Gateway, the Cambrian or the New Fifth Avenue hotels, and just when he was well on the way to being drunk for the rest of the night, they'd send over a vodka and orange juice courtesy of the RCMP. Although he appeared wide-eyed and paranoid to police, Colgan would guzzle down the screwdriver anyway. He wasn't one to turn down booze, especially if it were free.

The few times Lee did get worried, though, was when he received screwdrivers in the mail, usually at Christmas. They bore no return address but he must have known who they were from. The police, ever mindful of the murder weapon, preyed upon Lee, the weakest of the four.

CHAPTER EIGHT

In the early winter of 1972, Andrea Wiwcharuk, fourteen, was having a couple of beers at a trailer camp party with a date. She knew there was a party in The Pas just about every weekend and whether it was held in an abandoned house or at the Timberland Trailer Court, the kids did some heavy drinking.

Andrea was a little young to be going to drinking parties especially with a seventeen-year-old guy, but there she was, with about ten other people squeezed into a smoke-filled trailer. Andrea, a short, stout brunette, was sipping on half a glass of beer and listening to some rock music on the stereo when she heard Dwayne Johnston say out of the blue: "I picked up a screwdriver and I stabbed her and I stabbed her and I stabbed her." He stood facing Andrea making stabbing motions with his hands.

This little snippet of conversation caught her attention, as had the mime act, and she glanced up towards Johnston and the crowd circled around him. A few seconds passed, and then Johnston said, laughing, "They tore the car apart and we'll never get caught." Andrea was confused by what Johnston meant by all of this, and why the party guests, including Norm Manger, were having a good laugh over it; it didn't seem all that funny to her. Bewildered, Andrea looked over at Johnston, about six feet away, when she heard him say: "Do you know what it feels like to kill someone? It feels great.'' Then Johnston's girlfriend, Arlee White, told him to keep quiet and everyone seemed to settle down. Being as young as she was, Andrea didn't know what to make of Johnston's comments or what they meant, but they stuck in her mind. She left shortly afterwards because she had to be home by 11:00 P.M.

Although she told a friend about Johnston's statements some days later, she didn't mention them to the police for at least another thirteen years when they put out a public appeal.

Sixteen years after the party she repeated them before a Queen's Bench jury. Her testimony at the preliminary hearing was heavily criticized by Johnston's lawyer, Greg Brodsky, who was quick to point out that neither Manger nor Johnston could recall the party. Neither did Wiwcharuk's date. Brodsky asked her whether a $2,000 reward might have something to do with her sudden recall. Wiwcharuk denied receiving any money for her statement, explaining she hadn't gone to police right away because she hadn't realized the significance of Johnston's statements; she didn't know who he was talking about, either.

In 1973 Johnston moved to Red Deer, Alberta, to work for the city. Two years after that he moved to Calgary, and tried to start a small business with a friend. That didn't work out either and Johnston and his live-in girlfriend of five years, Arlee, moved to Kenora, where he was hired by Canadian Pacific Railways. Arlee, an average-looking, earthy, curly-haired blonde, landed a job at a nursing home and made friends with an attractive woman named Patricia Gauld, who was married at the time to a millworker named Terry.

By this time Arlee and Dwayne were having serious problems in their relationship; she was constantly accusing him of cheating on her, and subjected him to vigorous cross-examinations when he often came home late at night. Where were you? What were you doing? Are you screwing around on me? These were the first three questions put to Johnston as he staggered into the apartment and yanked off his fourteen-pound biker boots. It wasn't long before an irritated Johnston got fed up with the nightly third degree and simply told Arlee if she didn't like it, she knew where the door was.

Coincidentally, Patricia Gauld's marriage was also on the rocks in 1978. Patricia, twenty, a Ukrainian Catholic, had eloped with Terry, her first boyfriend, after dating him for about three years. After just eighteen months, Patricia realized Terry was too immature to be married, and she couldn't help wondering whether this sedentary existence was all that life held in store for her. Terry did have his qualities; he was handsome, well groomed, and mannerly. Sometimes Patricia would complain to Arlee about her failing marriage, only to watch her girlfriend's man, Dwayne, stop in to take her out for a spin on his Harley-Davidson.

There was something about Johnston that Patricia found strangely appealing. To her, Johnston represented everything that rebelled against society, especially her traditional, strict Catholic upbringing. Being the only girl in the family at the time, it was expected that she would remain a virgin until she married (she said she almost made it), and was taught that a woman's place is beside her man, the boss and breadwinner of the home. But that's exactly what Patricia was experiencing with Terry and she thought it dull. Johnston defied all convention. He had waist-length, chestnut-brown hair, and a long, scraggly beard; wore tattered blue jeans and big biker boots; and spoke his mind with his ranch-hand nasal twang. His nose looked as if it had been broken several times, and he had piercing sky-blue eyes neatly tucked under a well-ridged brow. He was rugged and macho – a frontiersman – and that intrigued her.

A tall, blue-eyed brunette with a girlish smile, Patricia had never met any one like Johnston. He was not one to flatter, but he would flirt. (That usually meant slapping a woman on her fanny.) He was an exciting, magnetic man, who could take Patricia away from the ordinary, staid life she had built in Kenora. Needless to say, her father didn't approve.

Patricia never confided to Arlee her interest in Johnston, but waited for her opportunity. First drinks, then she was in bed with him, running her fingers through his long hair and thinking how different the experience was from anything she had shared with her husband. Johnston didn't confide in Arlee right away, but told her to move out of the apartment: it was over. Patricia meanwhile separated from her husband and waited for the divorce Terry seemed as eager to get as she.

Johnston and Patricia didn't move in together right away. They had been going out for several weeks when Arlee made a surprise visit to Kenora from The Pas, saying she had to pick some things up she'd left behind. (A more likely reason for her visit was to attempt to get Johnston back.) Johnston happened to be home and hurriedly stuffed a few of Patricia's things under the bed as Arlee thumped on the door. Johnston let her in and followed behind as she stomped through the apartment, flipping through the closets for evidence of another female, in the guise of collecting her things.

Then Arlee made the mistake of lifting up the bedspread. Underneath were Patricia's shoes, socks, and underwear rolled up in a ball. Much as Johnston predicted, Arlee had a temper tantrum, screaming obscenities at him for screwing around on her with her friend. She threw Patricia's clothes all over the apartment.

Johnston managed to calm Arlee down and even negotiated one last weekend with her at the apartment. Monday morning, Patricia interrogated Johnston on where he had slept on the weekend, or rather whom he had slept with. Johnston methodically explained that Arlee had come to pick up a few of her things and ended up crashing on the couch. Patricia politely asked him to run that by her one more time. Johnston said he'd slept on the couch, no the bed – Arlee slept on the couch. "He always was a lousy liar," Patricia said later.

But Patricia shrugged off Johnston's last fling and moved in with him anyway. Johnston stayed a brakeman with CP Rail (coincidentally the same job Patricia's father held) and they fell in love, pledging to be together always. For Patricia, this was the man she'd always wanted – funny, bright, well read and sometimes romantic. For Johnston, Patricia was a beautiful, gentle, caring woman who wanted more than a dull life.

One day, Patricia recalls, Johnston said, "Honey, I love you so much, I'd love you to have my baby." Patricia rattled on in great detail that she had a $4,000 loan out; only $1,000 had been repaid. Having a kid would mean giving up her job at the Tasty Freez, and, while she loved him, it just wasn't financially feasible.

Johnston told her not to worry. Once she had the baby he would pay off the loan. He emphasized again how much he loved her and that he wanted the strong bond of a child, preferably a boy. His argument convinced Patricia to get off the pill, become pregnant, quit her job, and have a beautiful, blonde-haired, blue-eyed boy named Jeremia on May 11, 1979. Patricia often called Jeremia "My Man" and Dwayne "My Main Man."

By this time, Johnston had been transferred to Revelstoke, a picturesque town of about 8300, located in a valley in the southeast part of British Columbia. They rented a small house and settled into the quaint, little town. But Johnston didn't make all the payments on the loan and eventually Patricia was stuck with a lousy credit rating.

As soon as Johnston moved to Revelstoke, things seemed to change. No longer charming and romantic, he became miserly. He refused to buy her and the boy more than the minimum of clothing and he'd be curt with her if she spent more than the budgeted amount on groceries. (She got by with the family allowance cheques.) He took vacations alone, became bossy and aggressive and didn't like Patricia meeting other men – even his own biker friends. When they went out for drinks, he would often take her home early and go back to the bar alone. He never took her out for rides on his Harley, saying that if they got into an accident one-year-old Jeremia would be without a mom and dad. But Patricia suspected that Johnston's distrust of women went so deep that as much as he loved Patricia, he couldn't trust her absolutely.

Johnston had grown up with a mother who had several relationships with men after her marriage broke up. His mother was a hairdresser, who always seemed to have time for her dates and weekends with her boyfriends and for her son Darryl, a weak, soft man Dwayne described as a mama's boy. Perhaps she lost interest in her other children – Dwayne and his two sisters. More likely, she wanted to make up for the time she had lost in an unhappy marriage.

But the very qualities Johnston disliked in his mother were coming out in him. He had plenty of time for riding his Harley and drinking at the "clubhouse," a house some bikers bought to drink beer and indulge in other activities; but there was no time for Patricia – not even in bed – or for their son. As much as Johnston cared for them, he couldn't handle the responsibility.

Throughout the years, he often talked to her about his dream – to join The Rebels motorcycle gang in Saskatchewan. He liked the brotherhood. ("I told him I'm no biker lady and there's no way I would put up with that," Patricia recalled.) He routinely accused Patricia of cheating on him, even though she was at home with their baby boy while he was out all night and some weekends. She rationalized his behaviour: he was just unable to handle the responsibility of having a child; he would snap out of it eventually.

One day Patricia came up to Johnston as he was pulling on a Harley-Davidson T-shirt and she hugged him from behind. She pressed her cheek against his back and lifted up his beard to give him a kiss on the neck. There were two giant purple and green hickeys on his throat. "What the hell is this?" she asked. "I got in a fight last night and this guy came at my throat and tried to choke me," Johnston answered, seemingly convinced of his own argument.

Their relationship was snowballing into a disaster. Johnston was becoming increasingly aggressive, drinking more heavily and being more abusive to Patricia. She was getting tired of the whole charade; she had a kid and wanted to get her life together. During the summer of 1980 Patricia, Dwayne and "Brian," a tall, attractive friend and co-worker, went out for a few shooters and beers at a local bar. Patricia and Brian took a corner seat while Dwayne went up to the bar to get a few brews. They waited and waited. No Dwayne, no drinks. They scoured the bar for him, even checking the washrooms; but Dwayne must have found something else to interest him.

Brian and Patricia decided to drive around to look for Dwayne. (They had been attracted to each other when they first met several months earlier; but Brian was a married man and worked with Dwayne, and Patricia was determined never to cheat on Dwayne.) They had pretty well scoured just about every street in Revelstoke, gone to the clubhouse, bars, hotels and no Dwayne. All of a sudden Dwayne's infidelity, accusations and insults overwhelmed Patricia and she began to cry. Brian rubbed her back, and tried to soothe her pain.

After several hours of passion in the back of Brian's van, Patricia got home but Dwayne wasn't there and didn't return until the next morning. When Brian had asked to see her again, her conscience made her say no. She and Dwayne weren't getting along and he hadn't touched her for months; but she loved him and wanted to make it work. A week later she told him she had been unfaithful.

News of Patricia's infidelity, with a workmate of all people, sent Dwayne into a rage. He marched over to

Brian's house, thumped on the door, and screamed, "Come out here, you skinny son of a bitch." Brian calmly stepped out onto the porch, but before either could land a punch, Brian's wife jumped between them. Dwayne took a few seconds to size up Brian: the guy was a lot taller than Dwayne remembered and not quite as skinny. Dwayne walked away. A few days later, he was out for beers with Brian, joking, laughing, and blaming Patricia for the whole mess.

A year later due to the friction Patricia and Dwayne found each other's company insufferable. She was fed up with the abuse, his drinking and his smelling of stale beer, rye, and cigarettes every day. He was losing control and Patricia's face was often swollen and red. Patricia believed that Johnston was bordering on psychotic, he was so unpredictable, violent and vicious.

In 1981, a week before Christmas, Patricia moved to a transition house in Vernon about sixty miles southwest of Revelstoke. Two or three months later Dwayne arrived completely sober and promising things would be different. Desperately wanting to believe him, Patricia agreed to move back to Revelstoke. Before they knew it, Pat was pregnant. She had been on birth-control pills and was afraid of having a second child because of her first difficult delivery. Dwayne was quite pleased with Patricia's pregnancy and promised to go to prenatal classes with her, as he had for their firstborn, Jeremia.

Dwayne and Patricia made it through the prenatal classes and he helped by instructing her on breathing during labour, but his stomach was too weak to watch the birth. As tough as he acted, Patricia said Dwayne couldn't stand the sight of blood and walked out of the delivery room. On July 27, 1983, Patricia gave birth to another good-looking, blonde, blue-eyed baby. She was ecstatic.

About three weeks later, on August 18, 1983, relatives from both sides came to visit the couple in Revelstoke to take a look at baby Desiree. Dwayne decided that the time had come to get married. "We had everybody there and everything and I said, "Let's do it." The wedding wasn't formal; Patricia threw on a pink cotton dress with a blue sash, and Dwayne wore blue jeans, and a cut-off Harley-Davidson T-shirt, which revealed the tattoo on his upper left arm that spelled #1. They called a priest and said their vows in the back yard. He slipped a diamond ring on her finger and she a lion's-head ring on his. They stayed home caring for the baby for their honeymoon. "It wasn't a big deal to me," Dwayne recalled. "I loved her always and that never diminished."

In 1985, the happily married couple moved into their own three-bedroom, 1200-square-foot home, which had cost $52,000. Dwayne was making a good living as a brakeman and part-time conductor at CP Rail. He planned to pay off the mortgage by the time he was fifty-five.

A few months after his thirty-third birthday he was arrested for first-degree murder.

* * *

After the killing, it was a steady road downwards for Norm Manger. He drank and slept in dumpy hotel rooms in the glare of flashing neon signs. Norm didn't really belong anywhere or to anyone. His friends were measured by simple gestures such as turning over bar stools; their talk almost always revolved around drinking, and where to get more booze when the vendor was out. Friendships were superficial and short-lived; conversation would last until they were out of a wine. Other talk would revolve around life on the streets or scrounging for food, trying to remember what they had done the night before.

There was no routine to Norm's life except drinking night after night and intermittently working either as a bleacher for a mill or as a janitor.

Norm met Linda Hardy in 1982, in Cranbrook, a small town in southeast British Columbia surrounded by the Kootenay Mountains. Linda was sipping on a beer at the bar of the Cranbrook Hotel when she noticed a tall man, who looked Native, slouching at his stool. The short-haired, thirty-two-year-old brunette, who spoke with a lisp, began chatting to the man.

Linda was immediately attracted to Norm, who had long, thick, black shiny hair hanging gently off his shoulders. He had never been married, nor did he really care to do so, and he was very quiet and shy. "He sure is a nice guy," Linda recalled saying to herself.

Norm had suffered to a great degree from burnout, mostly caused by the heavy drinking he'd done over the years. But Linda didn't mind. "It was love at first sight for me," Linda recalled. "And we began seeing each other on and off for two years before we moved in together."

Norm talked to Linda about the past, which, for the most part, had been monotonous. He'd passed the time drinking, finding odd jobs, living in the street, sometimes paying a weekly rate at a third-rate hotel or crashing at a friend's house. It had been lonely, desperate and depressing.

Since his return to Cranbrook in 1982, he had hung around with Native people and taken up a job as a janitor and errand boy at a local print shop. The tall, thin man lived on the third floor of the Cranbrook Hotel and acquired a reputation as a quiet, peaceful guy.

Linda said Manger often mentioned The Pas. She said he was sentimental, recalling the good old times with his buddies, drinking and going to bars in the hustle and bustle of a town.

CHAPTER NINE

It started just two weeks after their marriage with a slap and a shove against the wall. Arlene never dreamed that her new husband, Lee Colgan, was capable of such a cowardly, pathetic act. Nor did Lee seem the type to hit a woman, at least not when he was sober. "When he was drunk it was like he became another person," Arlene recalled. "I learned to keep my mouth shut after the first time I was beaten."

The beatings began simply enough. Arlene, then twenty, would ask Lee where he had been until 2:00 A.M. as he staggered, reeking of rye and beer, into their trailer home. That seemed enough to push Lee over the edge and into a rage. He would grab Arlene by the shoulders and whip her against the wall, telling her it was none of her business and that she should shut up.

It wasn't too hard for Arlene to figure out where he had been, anyway. Lee spent most of his waking hours nursing a bottle of beer. "After two weeks it finally hit me that I was married to an alcoholic," Arlene recalled. When Lee wasn't too occupied with drinking, he'd be blowing joints, cruising with his friends around The Pas. Sometimes he worked as a brakeman. But most of that money, along with Arlene's wages as a waitress and later a telephone operator, went to nurse his habits. Usually there wasn't enough left to pay the rent or buy groceries, but Lee's parents often made up the difference. "They

always took care of him and I felt really bad about it —
he was a pampered boy,'' Arlene said.

When Lee was drunk, he was an ugly drunk, at least
to his wife. He was selfish, bad-tempered, argumentative,
self-pitying, and seemed to be consumed by rage. However, he never got into fights with men. Lee, then twenty,
was described by many of his friends as wimpy; if he
knew he'd lose a fight he wouldn't get involved. Instead
he would wait to take out his aggression on those who
were physically weaker, usually his wife.

And each time he woke from a drunken slumber after
hitting her, he'd apologize and promise to never do it
again. ''It's the booze doing it to me,'' Lee would say.
''I love you so much; I didn't mean to hurt you.'' A few
days would go by and he'd be at it again, this time with
more force. If Arlene asked, ''Are you drunk again?''
she'd earn herself a punch in the face. The query ''When
are you going to get off the booze and dope?'' assured
her a black eye and several weeks of explaining how
she'd walked into a door. After that, she stopped asking
questions; it became clear to her early on that Lee wasn't
about to change.

Arlene Karlenzig, a tall, thin, blue-eyed woman of
German descent with auburn hair, met Lee, not surprisingly, in a bar. She had been going to Keewatin Community College in The Pas for several months trying to
upgrade herself when she bumped into this mildly attractive, mousy-haired man who seemed so kind and
sincere. ''I just liked him,'' Arlene said, recalling their
first meeting. ''He was very kind and thoughtful and
seemed to genuinely care about people.''

They went out for three months before Lee popped the
question to Arlene on his parents' living-room couch.
Arlene was a sweet, naive girl with a strong maternal
instinct and grandiose ideas about what marriage would
be like, especially to a man from such a nice, respectable
family. ''I had these ideas about how a man and woman
should be close and communicate with each other and

that's what I expected," Arlene recalled. "My belief is that the man is the head of the house and a woman should be in submission. But to a point — she shouldn't be a doormat."

Her fairy-tale notions about relationships were shattered after two weeks, once they'd returned to The Pas from their honeymoon in Banff, Jasper, and Vancouver. They settled into a trailer at Timberland Trailer Court in late August 1973 but Lee wasn't prepared to give up his single life with his buddies at the bars. "He was seldom home," Arlene recalled. "And he was always spending all the money on booze. I would always get hit." Friends would tell Lee that his wife was a mouthy bitch, an airhead, and that she should learn to keep her trap shut.

She felt angry towards Lee for beating her but then began to feel sorry for this man who apologized so softly, so kindly, and lay his head in her lap. "I thought I could help him," Arlene recalled.

The first thing she tried was to get him away from his parents, who often paid the rent, who lent him the car he never put gas in, who babied him, and who were constantly at his beck and call. Getting him away from them might force Lee to be more independent and to accept responsibility, she reasoned.

A year later, in 1974, the couple moved to Lethbridge, Alberta, where his good friend Jim Houghton landed him a job selling smoke detectors. But he didn't last long at the job. "He went to work for a couple of days and decided to quit because he was frustrated. He didn't think he was doing well at it," Arlene said.

Shortly after that, the couple moved once again, this time to Fruitvale, British Columbia, a small town bordering Washington state, where her brother offered Lee a job selling Electrolux vacuum cleaners. He didn't do too badly at it, made a living, and genuinely seemed to be trying. But on March 24, 1975, Arlene was left alone when she gave birth to their first child, Scott Bruce James Colgan. Lee was apparently too busy or uninterested to see his firstborn, and drank at a bar all night. "I was in the hospital for six days and he only saw me once after my father dragged him out of a bar and forced him to see me and the baby," Arlene remembered. "The reality of it had hit him and he couldn't handle it."

The local town police in Fruitvale decided to take advantage of his demoralized situation. They knew from police in The Pas and other intelligence information they'd received that Lee had been involved in the 1971 murder of Betty Osborne and that he couldn't help talking about it when he was drunk and upset. After the birth of the Colgans' first child, a couple of plainclothes officers paid a visit to Lee in an effort to get him to confess to his role in the killing. Lee wasn't that weak, however, and he later complained that police were tormenting him by never letting him forget that horrible night.

Just a few days after the birth of his first son, Lee's apparent disinterest turned to boredom. He ignored them both, leaving his wife to do all the chores, the feeding, the cleaning and shopping alone.

It wasn't long before Lee found another excuse to quit his job selling vacuum cleaners, although he was doing quite well at it. After a little more than a year away from home, Lee complained of being homesick. "I don't know what it is about people from The Pas, but they just can't stand being away from there and Lee was one of them," Arlene recalled. The couple moved back to The Pas.

The party circuit in The Pas was hot and Lee was soon in the midst of it. Arlene, who desperately wanted to spend more time with Lee, started to hang out with his friends, too. One night at a party, when everyone was smoking dope, a friend of Lee's pulled her aside. "You are an embarrassment to Lee because you don't do drugs," she was told. Later on, Lee would say in court that he smoked dope, popped acid, and downed booze to erase the gruesome murder that had preyed on his mind every day of his life.

Police often paid visits to Arlene. "He just told me

he was there and with the wrong people at the wrong time,'' Arlene recalled. Arlene never suspected she was living with a killer. "I really believed him when he said that. Even though I know Lee has bouts of violence, I still don't think he did it.

"To be honest, what bothered me was that a girl had died. He told me he hadn't killed the girl and he went on and on about how it's upsetting his parents and his family. You know, I would think, 'You selfish, selfish guy,' and ask him, 'What about the girl's family?' ''

Over the years, Arlene confronted Lee many times about the killing, and asked him why he didn't go to the police and confess his involvement. "He told me for a long time that he was afraid," she said. "He said if he talked he would end up with a knife in his back. I'd say, 'Let's get it over with,' and he'd say he was afraid to speak. It ruined his life. He would just toss and turn at night. He would lie there awake. It bothered his conscience a lot. He said that was the reason he drank so much. It drove him.''

It was around 1976 when the couple separated; Arlene, who was again pregnant, took their son. "He wasn't interested anyway," she recalled. Lee promised to take her to the hospital and help during the birth despite their separation. "And I believed him," she said.

On May 22, 1976, Arlene went into labour. "I called Lee up and asked him if he could pick me up and he had some excuse, like his friends had a problem. I ended up having to take a cab to the hospital.''

The following day Arlene gave birth to Jennifer Leigh. The couple tried one last time to make it work in the fall of 1976. (Lee decided two kids were enough and got a vasectomy.) However, things were still rocky. "One day when Lee was at work, my mother came from B.C., and we loaded up everything and left him a note. Lee put out a missing person's report. Three months later I let him know where I was and that the children were safe.''
Shortly after their divorce, police were knocking at Lee's

door again, wanting answers about the murder of the Native girl.

A few weeks later, in early 1977, Lee wrote Arlene a threatening note at her home in Vernon. He blamed her for taking his only children away. "He said he'd kill me," Arlene recalled. "I think it was anger talking. He didn't mean it." But the threatening note proved handy. Arlene took it to a judge and was granted permanent custody of her kids. That letter would be used against Lee once more. In March 1987, Arlene would be called as a witness for the prosecution to testify against her ex-husband. But on the day of his preliminary hearing, he agreed to testify against two other men – Dwayne Johnston, who had already been arrested, and Jim Houghton, the good friend who had got him the job in Lethbridge. In exchange for his evidence, he was granted immunity.

Arlene remarried, to a Vietnam War veteran. Their son was born with a disorder of the nervous system that rendered him mentally handicapped. She divorced her husband after three years, because of his severe clinical depressions, and became a Jehovah's Witness.

Some time during the summer of 1977 or 1978 – he can't remember which – Lee was drinking in the Royal Canadian Legion with sheriff Gerald Wilson of The Pas. An RCMP officer, desperate to provoke a confession, sent over a vodka screwdriver. Drunk and upset, Lee told Wilson that he thought the Mounties were trying to drive him crazy. The sheriff invited him out for a chat in his camper parked on the street.

Colgan said later in court that he told the sheriff "pretty well everything" about the killing. "He [Wilson] told me about the shit he could get me in cause he was the sheriff," Lee said in court. The RCMP said it wasn't until 1986 that Wilson told police about the conversation. Wilson has refused to comment about the incident.

In 1979, Lee was drinking at the Legion with friend Steve Maksymetz, then thirty-seven. "He was asking me what is it that makes me able to carry on with life,"

Maksymetz said. Embroiled in a bitter divorce after his wife stabbed him with a knife, he'd just become a born-again Christian and began sharing the good word with Colgan. "I told him it was the power of Jesus Christ that helped and he started talking to me about the murder and I told him, 'I know about it – everybody in town knows about it.' " Lee asked what he should do. "I told him the best thing to do was to confess it because it's going to haunt you for the rest of your life." But Lee didn't take his buddy's advice. Maksymetz says he didn't go to the police because he thought they already knew about it and, if they didn't, it wasn't his responsibility to tell them.

The years between 1979 and 1986 were much the same for Lee. He drank, worked occasionally as a drywaller, continued his drug trafficking, tried unsuccessfully to quit drinking several times and was sought out by police many times regarding the murder.

In the summer of 1986, he started living with thirty-five-year-old Evelyn Daily shortly after the death of her common-law husband, Richard Morrissette. On his deathbed Morrissette had asked Lee to look after Evelyn. After a few weeks of living together, Lee told Evelyn that the police wanted him for murder. "He said the police would start harassing me about a murder he was involved in because I was going out with him," Evelyn said. "He told me what had happened, that he and some other guys had picked up a girl, they had taken her out to the lake and the one guy had killed her. He didn't say names but said that he wasn't involved – that he had nothing to do with it other than being in the car when they had picked her up." At that point Evelyn asked him to go to the police and confess, but he refused. Evelyn said she didn't go to police because it wasn't her place and she wasn't sure if she could even believe Lee because he'd been so drunk and drugged-up. Evelyn hadn't heard rumours of the murder, she says, because she had only lived in The Pas for three years by the time Lee confessed to her. She didn't press the matter after Lee told her it would only be a matter of time before police caught up with him.

After four months of cohabitating, Evelyn was fed up with Lee and his $200-a-week cocaine, marijuana and alcohol habits. Lee had already weasled $5,000 from Evelyn for drugs, booze, food and rent – money she earned working at the Gateway Hotel. During the last few weeks of their relationship, Evelyn's interest was focused on Steve Maksymetz. Within a few weeks they began living together. Lee confronted Steve and told him that Evelyn was his and that he loved her. Steve told Lee he hadn't taken her away, but that she was just sick of Lee.

Days later, Steve woke up to find his pick-up truck vandalized: the mirrors, headlights, and body had been smashed. A friend told him he'd seen a man, who fit the description of Lee Colgan, bashing the truck with a crow-bar the night before. Steve called the RCMP to report the vandalism but they told him they couldn't investigate it. "They said they didn't want to stir up any shit because there was a big investigation going on." Two weeks later, on October 3, 1986, Lee was arrested for first-degree murder at his parents' 753 Constant Avenue home. He was put in hospital instead of jail because he was suffering from delirium tremens, a symptom of advanced alcoholism.

* * *

The proposal wasn't anything elaborate or formal, but Shannon Leslie White said yes, she would marry James Robert Paul Houghton. The pair did just that on October 5, 1974 in The Pas. There was no honeymoon; the two needed to save all the money they could. Shannon was almost seven months pregnant.

Shannon, an attractive vivacious brunette, was from a large family and had always dreamed of marrying the boy next door. (In fact, Jim lived down and across the street.) Ever since she was fourteen, Shannon had had a crush on Jim, although he was twenty-one then and would hardly have been interested in a kid. Like many young men in The Pas, he would have been sowing his wild oats.

As soon as Jim slipped the wedding band on, he fulfilled all of Shannon's wishes: a comfortable home and a family to put in it. Shannon was a woman with simple tastes, content to make a home and life with friends, family and her man, the head of the household.

So when she heard those awful rumours about the killing of a Native girl years earlier (when she had been about fifteen or sixteen) it didn't occur to her that her groom might be involved. He seemed like such a nice, likable guy, hardly the type. As she puts it: "It just never came up and it was something I never really thought about. I remember hearing some girl got killed and it was like water off a duck's back to me."

Shortly after their marriage, the pair moved to Lethbridge, where Jim got a job selling smoke detectors. It would never make them rich, but they would get by. Shannon gave birth to James Jr., on December 26, 1974. Jim was there all through labour and the birth. He was pleased as pie.

Jim was a good provider – responsible, reliable, practical and even-tempered, sometimes too good-tempered. "Even when we had arguments he wouldn't yell," Shannon recalled. "He'd say, 'You don't have to yell. I'm right in front of you.' He was the one who was quiet. It's me who gets more riled at times and yells at him. People say it's those kind of people you have to watch out for, the kind who hold everything inside, but I don't think there was another side to Jim. If there was, I never saw it."

The only side Shannon saw or cared to see was the nice, easy-going Jim, who friends say, wouldn't hurt a fly, as he was decent, caring, and generous to a fault. He was entertaining – the classic clown at times – and he'd give you the shirt off his back.

Jim, Shannon and James Jr., lived in an apartment in Lethbridge for some time. A second child, Darren, arrived on November 26, 1976. "I just didn't want to have any more," Shannon recalled. "I was happy having two boys."

Shannon loved Jim; he loved her. They wanted a house, kids, and a nice, comfortable retirement. Vacations were trips down to the United States or to British Columbia, and going back to The Pas every summer.

There, Shannon would visit her six sisters and chat about the usual things – cooking, cleaning, men, husbands, and kids. (Her sister, Arlee, was then living with Dwayne Johnston.) Jim would buddy around with five or six friends, including Lee Colgan. They'd talk about the good old days, drinking at the Gateway or the Cambrian, or the heyday of the mill, which was in a steady decline by the late 1970s. There probably wasn't too much talk about the killing of Betty Osborne. People never questioned Jim about it because it seemed unbelievable that such a nice guy could have been involved.

In 1976, Conrad Lamb was cleaning the outhouse out at the Houghton cabin. A dark-coloured jacket jammed up his pump. He tossed aside the mucked-up garment, and thought little about it until some years later, when he mentioned it to the police. It was never positively identified, but police suspected it was the jacket Betty Osborne was wearing the night of the murder – the jacket they never recovered.

It was around 1977 that Jim started a new job as an industrial salesman with Hilti, a construction-parts firm. The job would allow him to move up in the world. He was hired because of his solid background selling smoke detectors and he was given the sales territory of Lethbridge, Medicine Hat, and southern Alberta. He immediately impressed his boss, Charlie Russell, as a happy, easy-going fellow. "We didn't have any problems with him and he did his job," Russell recalled. "He was an average salesman."

Around 1979, the family bought a duplex, and settled in until they were able to afford a single-family house. In 1985, they moved into a four-bedroom house in a subdivision on the west side of Lethbridge, right across from the river.

It was around then that Jim had become one of four prime suspects being investigated for the murder of Helen Betty Osborne, a possibility he'd probably never even considered after all these years. And if he had his way, his wife wouldn't consider it, either. He didn't mention it to her, and she, not the one to challenge her man, says she never thought to ask him about it.

Shannon remains completely and blindly devoted to Jim. Her marriage, she says, is great. "We have problems, but the same kinds all other couples have. We're pretty ordinary for the most part."

Jim helped coach his two sons on the minor-league hockey team in Lethbridge; he gladly babysat and took care of other people's kids. He impressed Diane Alstad, a friend and neighbour, when she met him in September 1983. "They were the first people we met and I was a single parent then and they had me down for barbecues and were very good to me," recalled Diane, a former probation officer. "He was very easy-going, fun-loving and dedicated to his family and would do anything for his kids. He was a hard worker, reliable and his job was self-motivated."

Diane said that the one thing that impressed her about Jim was that he never seemed to lose his cool. "Apparently a few boys were in his van and throwing gum or something at each other and he let them have a good time," Diane recalled. "My husband couldn't believe it. He said if that had been him, he would have killed them."

CHAPTER TEN

"This is an amazing case, yet you can't get it into court. Why?" RCMP constable Bob Urbanoski asked a fellow officer. Urbanoski had just taken over the officer's desk in the general investigative section in Thompson in late 1982 and with it came the thirty or so volumes and files and police statements stamped Helen Betty Osborne.

For the past eleven years the case had been passed from officer to officer in The Pas and then sent farther north to the Thompson investigative section to see if officers there could find a way, usually in their spare time, to get the case into court. No one could, and the files sat collecting dust.

The problem, of course, had nothing to do with who the killers were, or even where they could be located; that was all easy enough. One was in The Pas, the second in Lethbridge, the third in Revelstoke, and the fourth in Cranbrook – all of them listed in the phone book for easy access. There was no clear-cut physical evidence linking the four to the killing, however, and, as the years dragged on, the trail got colder.

Urbanoski, a constable with seven years' experience, had been transferred to the Thompson city detachment from Lac du Bonnet, Manitoba, in 1979 and moved on to the general investigative section as a plainclothes officer four years later.

The twenty-nine-year-old man of Ukrainian descent

RCMP Constable Bob Urbanoski (photo: Lisa Priest)

RCMP Constable Don Knight

never would have dreamed that he would be working on one of the toughest and oldest homicides in the province. He had dropped out of school halfway through grade twelve, and had wanted to join the police years earlier, partly because of its job security. But at five foot nine and a half he was half an inch too short to qualify for the city forces, and because he was married he couldn't join the RCMP, either. So he worked as a travelling electronics salesman and a truck driver in Winnipeg until he heard the RCMP had changed its rules and was hiring married men. Finally, in 1975, Urbanoski was sworn in as a constable in training.

When he looked over the Betty Osborne file in late 1982, he immediately became fascinated with it, and in July 1983 he was officially assigned the case. "I would ask myself, what's wrong with this picture, where's the problem?" Urbanoski recalled. "I always felt that we've got to be able to take it to court; there's just too much there. There's got to be some way to charge these guys."

It was unlike any other unsolved murder in the province. Physical evidence showed that at least one person, but probably more, had stabbed and beaten Betty Osborne and at least two had dragged her into the bushes. Court testimony later showed that four men had been at the scene, but which ones had done it? Had she been stabbed with just one screwdriver or the two seized near the scene?

About two hundred cops had looked through the case over the years, but none would be put on it full-time until Urbanoski's assignment in December 1984. Urbanoski's only job would be to review the case and try to get it into court, no matter how long it took or how much it cost. It had to be solved.

The case had become an embarrassment to the RCMP. Everyone north of the 53rd parallel knew who had been involved in the killing of Osborne, and justice hadn't been done. After all, this was no contract killing, or even the work of a scheming, devious mind. Four unsophisticated local boys had left behind the murder weapon and hadn't even bothered to clean out the car. However, a murder of this stature could no longer be kept on the back burner.

Urbanoski spent his first six months on the case making inquiries around The Pas, sifting through police statements, and trying to fill in the blanks in the killer's lives over the past thirteen years. There would be a lot to consider after all that time. Two men, Johnston and Houghton, had done very well for themselves and were now leading reasonably stable lives with their families.

A more likely suspect was Colgan, a failed drug trafficker, alcoholic, divorcee, and wife beater who constantly talked about the killing. Manger, too, seemed a likely suspect, considering he'd made a life of trying to wash away all those years with booze. Then again, he had the reputation of being a timid, frightened man.

Then there was the question of motive. Killers almost always know their victims. Had any of the four men in the car that night known Betty Osborne? Years later on the witness stand, Colgan denied knowing her. But her former boyfriend, Cornelius, who had attended the same school as Lee for four years, recalled that the three had been together on several occasions. Colgan was known around town for going out with Native women and he had told more versions of the killing than he would probably care to recall. He had threatened to kill his wife, and wouldn't think twice about hitting a woman. He certainly seemed capable of murder. Why didn't he just go to police? They were ready and waiting. His fear of Johnston certainly couldn't have been Colgan's only reason not to talk. Had he played a large role in it? What was he really afraid of?

Johnston, too, had a lot going against him. He was a tough guy, a braggart, and knew several men connected to the Rebels motorcycle gang, listed by police intelligence across Canada as a dangerous criminal organization that had been trying to become associated with the California-based Hell's Angels. Police heard rumours that Johnston had killed an Indian man in a car accident in The Pas and supposedly bragged about it. As well, there were rumours that Johnston used to beat his wife, Patricia, and former girlfriend, Arlee White; but both women denied it to police. He was also known for not co-operating with police. There was already at least one RCMP officer who didn't like him and had thought him the killer ever since his early days in The Pas. That officer warned Johnston it was just a matter of time until they pinned the murder on him.

Although he, too, fit the image of the killer, there were a couple of things that didn't quite make sense. He wore size 8 1/2 shoes, smaller than the others and not as likely to have left those imprints in the snow. As well, as much as he appeared to dislike Natives, he, for the most part, remained indifferent to Native women. He also didn't used to hang around with the three others. Why would he have been with them?

Then there was Houghton. He was good friends with Colgan and too cool for his own good. He was also strong. A jacket that had likely been Osborne's was found stuffed down the outhouse at his cottage, and word had it that Native girls had visited him there on weekends. Whatever his role, had he kept his mouth shut because he realized the consequences of any involvement? Police also tried to locate a man Houghton had allegedly confessed the killing to while vacationing in Las Vegas. After a lengthy search, they finally found the man but he denied that the conversation had taken place.

Houghton was the ultimate mystery man, probably the most fascinating of the four. Here was a guy who had been involved in a brutal murder, and yet everyone thought he was such a nice, sweet family man. He coached minor hockey teams and was the epitome of the community man.

Then there was Manger, a drunk and a vagrant. A

witness who testified later at the trial said Manger had laughed when Johnston bragged at the party that the four men wouldn't get caught for the murder. What was he trying to hide?

Urbanoski definitely had his work cut out for him. But the fact that the RCMP had waited so many years to make the murder a number-one priority left Urbanoski saddled with some unfortunate problems. Phillip McGillivary, the cab driver who had been hypnotized one month after the killing and remembered four of six digits on the death car's licence plate, died of old age in the late 1970s. Death had robbed the Crown of a key witness who had seen the car leave the murder scene.

His second biggest problem was that the only man who presumably knew all the answers to the murder was the lawyer D'Arcy Bancroft. At the age of thirty, in 1974 he died in his sleep at a hotel in southern California while attending a cat-lover's convention. He had suffered a stroke several months before his death. His law partners destroyed his files after his death and Bancroft took whatever he knew to the grave with him.

One more aspect Urbanoski would have had to consider was a strangely similar unsolved murder that had occurred north of Kenora. In June 1974, the nude body of Ojibwa Indian Susan Assin, nineteen, was found wearing only socks. She'd been stabbed in the chest. There was no murder weapon and no evidence of sexual assault. She had been a resident of Grassy Narrows Indian Reserve. No one was ever charged for the crime.

Urbanoski immediately began looking at new police methods, such as foreign hair transfers and genetic blood tests. But even they couldn't work on thirteen-year-old evidence. Urbanoski had no more to work with in 1983 than police had had twelve years earlier, except a limitless budget, co-operation from the Attorney General's department, help from dozens of other officers across Canada, and hindsight. Screwdriver drinks, countless visits to the suspects, and confrontations hadn't worked. The four men had to be provoked, even if indirectly, and they had to be monitored.

And the best way of doing that was to get wiretaps on the phones and state-of-the-art listening devices installed in the basements of the men's homes that could pick up conversations from all rooms. Both wiretaps and such devices can only be used in police investigations if a Queen's Bench judge is satisfied that all other investigating methods have failed. They are usually only given for a sixty-day period. Pillow talk, noisy love-making sessions, family fights – every aspect of daily family life would also be recorded because the device worked twenty-four hours a day. As well, visiting the men's relatives, placing public appeals in newspapers, and resorting to other methods of persuasion would have to be employed. Police must have known this was the only way to get the four men and the town of The Pas to talk about a murder that had happened thirteen years earlier.

In late June 1985, Urbanoski placed this ad in the bi-weekly the *Opasquia Times*:

The RCMP are requesting the public's assistance in the investigation of a murder which occurred over 13 years ago.

On Saturday, November 13, 1971, the body of Helen Betty Osborne, 19, was found near Clearwater Lake. Osborne, a resident of The Pas and formerly of Norway House, had been attending school in The Pas at the time of her murder.

She was last seen alive at about 2:00 a.m. near the corner of Third St. and Edwards Ave. on the morning of her death. Police believe she had been lured into a vehicle and then taken to the Clearwater Lake area where she was brutally murdered.

A light-coloured automobile with Manitoba licence plates was seen in the area where the body was located at the time the murder was believed to have been committed.

An RCMP spokesman said yesterday police have had a terrific response from the public on the case to date, but they are looking for more help from people in The Pas and the surrounding area.

'We're not looking for a big break in the case,' he said, adding police would like to hear anything about the incident people may have seen or heard. 'No matter how trivial it is, we'd like to hear it . . . sometimes we can use bits of information to tie things together.'

The spokesman said people may have been afraid to come forward with information at the time, intimidated by peer pressure, or may even have thought their information too insignificant to mention. Police are even interested in learning the names of people who may know something about the incident.

The last two paragraphs assured confidentiality and listed a telephone number.

Just about everyone in The Pas read that advertisement and gossip about the murder was as rife as it had been fourteen years earlier. Friends and families of the four men were concerned about the ad and wondered who was going to be charged with the murder. Even Sheriff Wilson mentioned to The Pas Crown Attorney Dan Dutchin that Colgan had told him what happened, in his camper truck several years earlier. Dutchin told Wilson he must go to the police with the information immediately. Just to make sure, Dutchin contacted R.C.M.P. officers and told them what he had heard.

But the tapes recorded by the listening devices only contained vague generalities. According to bail transcripts, the police had the wiretaps rolling when Johnston had these telephone conversations.

On June 25, 1985, an associate of Johnston's in The Pas telephoned him at his Revelstoke home. Johnston wanted to know if there was a possibility of talking to anyone in the area. The associate replied that he was still keeping an eye on the area; he felt that everyone had moved away years ago but that someone must have been talking. He told Johnston he would keep in touch if anything developed on his end in The Pas. (The pair were supposedly discussing the murder investigation.)

On July 15, 1985, someone higher up in the Rebels motorcycle gang telephoned Johnston and talked to him about the recent police activity in The Pas since the police had reopened the investigation of Betty Osborne's murder. Johnston felt that someone in The Pas had a ''loose lip.'' The associate was planning on being in The Pas in three days and agreed to do some checking around on Johnston's behalf. He also said he could make a telephone call that might straighten a few things out for Johnston.

On August 6, 1985, another associate of Johnston's met with him in his Revelstoke home. A recording device installed in his basement some time earlier recorded their conversation during which Johnston told his associate how he'd helped others collect an outstanding debt in Calgary. He described the debt as a ''ripoff.'' The debt had been collected by means of threats and intimidation; articles of property as well as two hundred dollars in cash had been taken from a friend who had been at the residence at the time. Johnston mentioned that although he was a little guy ''he scared'' people because of his looks.

On December 6, 1985, a friend from The Pas told Johnston about a ''Crime Stoppers'' article that had appeared in the local paper less than six months after it had been published. Both were concerned about the article and the possible reaction to it. The friend agreed to take care of things from his end for Johnston.

We do not know now – nor may we ever – how police managed to install wiretaps and state-of-the-art recorders in at least three of the four men's homes for such a long period of time. A six-inch-thick document containing the transcripts of wiretap conversations against Johnston didn't yield much.

Johnston's phone was tapped for three years in fact. A letter from the Attorney General's department informed him in 1986 of the duration and listed the various dates Crown attorneys had applied for extensions. Such surveillance is unusually long, considering most applications are only granted on a sixty-day basis and extensions can usually only be acquired for an extra thirty days. The letter also informed him he had been under police surveillance for several years.

Dwayne and his wife Patricia suspected their telephone was being bugged because of the loud clicks and background voices. "Sometimes we'd swear into the phone or say something back to the police, to let them know we knew." Patricia recalled. Others times, Dwayne and his friends would talk in code language, but the cops knew what they were talking about.

The Houghton family also suspected their phone was being tapped as well as their home and often teased the police about it. "When we were in bed, we'd be goofy and say things like: 'You want to get your money's worth?' " Shannon Houghton recalled. Manger was the only one of the four suspects who was not recorded.

During the winter of 1985 Urbanoski was making the rounds and talking to the relatives of the four men when he visited Bill Brown, Patricia Johnston's uncle who lived in Winnipeg. Apparently, Urbanoski convinced Brown that Johnston was the likeliest man to have killed Osborne. Brown, in turn, called Patricia. "He [Brown] tried to convince me I was living with a murderer and I was lucky it wasn't me," Patricia recalled. Urbanoski also interviewed Patricia's mother and told her Johnston was their man, adding it was only a matter of time before they got him.

The news of her uncle's interview and the murder investigation frightened Patricia. She demanded that

Johnston tell her what was going on since the police were listening in on their conversations. She had no clue about Johnston's involvement in the murder. "He said he didn't know what was going on," she later reported.

As more friends and relatives of the murder suspects were interviewed, some telephoned the suspects to inform them about what police were saying. None of the men would admit to anything, so that the police had no incriminating evidence on tape to charge them with or to take to court.

Urbanoski called Johnston long distance at his Revelstoke home at one point in 1985, apparently to make an appointment for an interview. "I hung up on him," Johnston recalled. "Then he called me again and said, 'You don't hang up on me,' and I hung up on him again." The police must have been getting more suspicious about Johnston's role in the murder, especially since he was the only one of the four who was blatantly unco-operative with the Mounties. Johnston said he didn't take the calls that seriously and, besides he never talked to cops.

Altogether Urbanoski travelled to about fifty cities from Toronto to Vancouver and made between one hundred and fifty to two hundred inquiries about the murder. He memorized every date, every fact, and was determined to see justice done. But the wiretaps hadn't yielded nearly as much as police had anticipated.

The public appeal had helped, but they hadn't received a great deal of information. Judging from the one hundred and fifty calls they had received, it became very apparent that Colgan had told many, many people in The Pas that he had been involved in the killing. It also appeared that neither Houghton nor Manger had told anyone about the murder, at least anyone that had gone to police.

One very helpful piece of information police did get was supplied by Andrea Wiwcharuk. In 1985 she told the police about the incident at the trailer-camp party thirteen years earlier when she had heard Johnston brag about the killing and boast about how great it felt to kill someone. This would be some of the most damning evidence later presented at the trial.

Police had made some progress but they knew they needed more. They had to get someone to talk about the killing. The only way they could do that was to go after the weakest man of the four.

CHAPTER ELEVEN

Urbanoski swooped down on Lee Colgan at his parents' home and arrested him for first-degree murder on October 3, 1986.

Colgan was taken in manacles to The Pas detachment just before 8:00 A.M. where he was booked and had his mug shot taken. Although Colgan had tried dozens of times over the years to quit drinking, his mug shot showed the toll booze had taken. Ravaged by years of drug and alcohol abuse, it would only be a matter of hours before he went into convulsions and then withdrawal in the absence of his usual beer or Carrington's rye for breakfast.

Slightly slurring his speech, Colgan telephoned his lawyer, Donald MacIver, a sharp, somewhat cantankerous man who had been practising law for twenty-nine years. But despite his experience, he thought that the charge sounded bizarre. Somehow the gossip about the murder had managed to slip by him. "Who's been killed?" MacIver wondered, still half asleep in his bed. "Some Indian girl fifteen years ago?"

Hearing Colgan's garbled words convinced MacIver that his client was hung over and he rushed down to The Pas detachment to see him. Colgan was in rough shape. MacIver suspected that Urbanoski's method was to make Lee go cold turkey, hoping he'd reveal what he knew about the murder. If this was some sort of police technique, it wasn't going to work. And MacIver let

Urbanoski know it from the outset with one blunt, challenging question. "I asked who would be looking after him with his DTs and convulsions, basically because I said I wanted to know who we were going to sue," MacIver recalled.

His question apparently scared Urbanoski enough to allow Colgan to be hospitalized under guard until his bail hearing, six days later. At the hospital, MacIver explained what could happen to Colgan – if he was convicted of first-degree murder, he could count on receiving twenty-five years before being eligible for parole. MacIver knew Colgan wouldn't live through one year of prison, let alone twenty-five, if he was convicted of killing an innocent Native woman with a screwdriver. He'd be dead in no time.

Just before the bail hearing on October 9, MacIver visited the Crown attorney's office in The Pas to inform Daniel Dutchin that he wanted total immunity or nothing. Dutchin made a mental note of it and didn't oppose Colgan's release during the hearing.

At the hearing itself, MacIver stressed to Justice K. Hanssen that Colgan was a townsperson with a job as a drywaller; he lived with his parents who were respected in the community, and wouldn't flee The Pas should he be granted bail. Justice Hanssen said he was concerned about how the community would react to having a man with a first-degree murder charge in its presence. He asked MacIver for his comments.

"Well, My Lord, we can't stop the newspapers from their sensationalism, but I think, My Lord, that the position which will be taken throughout it is, yes, unequivocally this girl was murdered. For instance, the newspaper [the *Opasquia Times*] has carried on about a rape and certainly there's no evidence of any sexual offence so vicious as a rape or anything taking place . . . The other thing, however, the denial is there and the denial will be throughout; that Lee Scott Colgan did not and underline the word not murder this girl."

MacIver also pointed out to the court that with the exception of one impaired driving charge, Colgan had had a clean record. Colgan was freed on a $50,000 surety, which his parents obtained by mortgaging their home. The other conditions of his release were that he report Mondays, Wednesdays, and Fridays to the RCMP detachment in The Pas and that he stay in Manitoba. He was also required to abstain from alcohol and take counselling for alcoholism at Rossaire House, a detoxification centre.

Arlene Demmings was worried when she heard news of her ex-husband's arrest and called the Thompson RCMP to ask Urbanoski if he really believed Lee was the killer. "He said, 'We know Lee wasn't actually the one who used the screwdriver but we think that . . . [arresting him] . . . will scare him enough to get him talking.' " Demmings recalled.

MacIver knew it too. "The Crown knew that without my client's evidence, they really had very little chance of getting anybody," MacIver recalled. "They didn't want him [Colgan] – they knew it was a power play. But my client had no reason not to cooperate completely with the police. But his price was immunity."

The Crown held out. Three weeks later, the police finally had enough evidence to arrest Dwayne Johnston – the man they had wanted all along. Two RCMP officers from Thompson and some others from Revelstoke roared up to Johnston's home on the afternoon of October 26 and surrounded every exit.

Johnston, then thirty-three, was leisurely working on a motorcycle in his basement with two friends, while his three-year-old daughter, Desirée, watched. Then they heard the sirens blaring. "I said, Holy shit, this is just like *Miami Vice*," recalled Brad Powell, Johnston's friend. "There were police everywhere, every door."

Powell said that the police stormed downstairs and he grabbed Desiree and held her up to his chest. The police, unsure of what Powell would do, drew their guns on him, he said. ''I guess they thought I was going to take her hostage. It was really wild. He [Johnston] was plucked and all of a sudden he's gone. There must have been twelve cops there.''

Johnston asked police if he could give his daughter a goodbye kiss but they refused and slapped the cuffs on him.

Powell took Desiree back to his home and then called Patricia at work, telling her to get over to his house right away because something awful had happened. Patricia, concerned there was something wrong with Desiree, rushed to Powell's home to find him sitting on the couch, his face white. ''I told her Dwayne had been picked up on a first-degree murder charge and she flipped,'' Powell recalled.

Patricia was a bag of nerves. She was crying and shaking, and took what she called ''mellow'' pills, some mild tranquillizers sold in drugstores. ''Then I went to the jail with a bag of clothes and this officer told me he was really sorry but that I'd have a long road ahead of me,'' Patricia recalled. ''Then he asked if Dwayne ever hurt me, threatened me, and wanted to know what his personality was like.''

Distraught, Patricia told the officer quite convincingly that Dwayne had never hurt her and said she wanted to see her husband. She went into the interview room and talked to Johnston through a glass barrier. ''He was totally shocked and all I could do was cry,'' she recalled. ''Then I said to him, 'You tell me what the hell is going on here' and he said he didn't know.''

Patricia said her husband seemed dumbstruck; he was shocked he had been arrested. Apparently he hadn't taken Urbanoski's earlier inquiries about the murder too seriously.

For days, Patricia was fraught with worry. She didn't know how to break the news to her kids that their father wouldn't be home for a long, long time. At first, she told an inquisitive Jeremia that Dwayne was visiting friends in Saskatoon. She herself had a great deal of difficulty believing her husband when he said he didn't know what was going on. "Then why are you here?" she would ask him.

A few days after the arrest, Patricia's mother came from Winnipeg and helped organize her finances. Patricia went on welfare and lowered her mortgage payments. Within a few months, she had lost everything to pay the legal bills: the house, the furniture, the car – anything of value – and eventually received legal aid. She subsequently moved to Winnipeg to be closer to her parents and her husband, who was to be imprisoned at the downtown Remand Centre.

Dwayne Johnston appeared for his bail hearing several times before it was finally heard. "When I saw him come into The Pas [from Revelstoke] I couldn't believe it," one lawyer said. "He looked like a Mountain man." Johnston's lawyer, Greg Brodsky, however, did a pretty good job of cleaning his client up. Johnston's waist-length hair, six-inch beard, and Harley T-shirts disappeared. He looked like a choir boy when he appeared in pastel-coloured shirts.

Senior Crown Attorney George Dangerfield and Greg Brodsky argued about the location for the bail hearing. Dangerfield wanted it heard in The Pas, but Brodsky preferred Winnipeg. There were several remands before it was finally heard in Winnipeg on November 20, 1986.

Dangerfield argued that Johnston should be denied bail because he had attempted to hamper the police investigation, associated with motorcycle gang members, and was willing to use their "services" if need be. He also described Johnston as an extremely dangerous man who threatened people and used violence to his own ends. Dangerfield pointed to his criminal record, which he described as trivial, but typical of Johnston's behaviour: Johnston had been convicted and fined first in 1973 for obstructing a peace officer, again in 1974 for common assault, and then in 1981 for mischief. (He had fired a few shots from one of his rifles into the air outside his home in celebration of the American hostages' release in Iran.)

Dangerfield also told the court that a witness would testify at the trial about what she had overheard Johnston tell some party guests in the winter of 1972 and that he had made the statement, "I picked up a screwdriver and I stabbed her and I stabbed her and I stabbed her."

Brodsky in turn argued that the Crown's evidence was not trustworthy and that Johnston didn't accept it. Even though Johnston might have had associates who belonged to a "motorcycle club," as Brodsky put it, he had never asked them to do anything illegal or unethical in the taped telephone conversations. Johnston had never said he had been involved in the murder, Brodsky added.

Wary about Johnston's affiliations with motorcycle gangs and the danger to the public interest, Justice Guy J. Kroft denied Brodsky's request for bail. The decision wasn't appealed.

In stark contrast to the testimony to be given one year later at the murder trial, Dangerfield briefly outlined the Crown's evidence against Colgan at Johnston's bail hearing. Oddly enough, the Crown had not outlined this argument at Colgan's bail hearing.

Dangerfield said that Colgan had been driving his father's car on the night of November 12, 1971, in an attempt to pick up Betty Osborne. That night he ended up in the company of three other men; they drove Osborne out to the airport and started to tear off her clothes in an attempt to have sex with her. When Osborne fought them off vigorously, they tried to force her and when that didn't work, they beat her. Colgan said she had been killed at the airport because she wouldn't "screw" for the men and that the dead body had been taken across the road to the pumphouse area where it was dumped into the bushes. This was one story Colgan had supposedly told several people in The Pas.

Colgan's testimony at the trial, however, was completely different from the story he had told the Crown.

In his testimony he cast all the blame for Osborne's death on Johnston and Houghton. But it was a difficult story to believe. Defence lawyers suggested that it had been rammed into his head by the Crown. Colgan had in fact told several different versions of the killing. "I mean, I don't know what happened that night," one lawyer on the case remarked. "I don't think we ever will."

On March 10, 1987, Colgan and Johnston were to attend a preliminary hearing to determine whether there was enough evidence to commit them to stand trial. Judge Robert Trudell in The Pas, who reportedly shouts at the accused during sentencing, was to hear the arguments.

But minutes before the preliminary hearing was to begin, Dangerfield and MacIver were meeting behind closed doors. The atmosphere was tense. The doors to the interview room were being slammed, desks were being cleared, and raised voices could be heard echoing through the provincial court building while clerks cautiously tiptoed through the hallways. Several times that day, Colgan was dragged in, given a going-over and told to wait. Witnesses scheduled to appear stood idle, shuffling their feet in the hallways.

Dangerfield must have known that without Colgan he'd be unlikely to get Johnston convicted and he needed someone to turn hard evidence. MacIver let him know this, too. "George [Dangerfield] wanted my client to plead to a crime and the answer was no," MacIver recalled. "It was all or nothing and it was take it or leave it."

Dangerfield obviously chose to leave it for several hours. He told MacIver he wanted Colgan to plead guilty to accessory after the fact – the only thing the criminal director of prosecutions at the time, Wayne Myshkowsky, would accept. This was the second round of bargaining. Three months earlier, in December 1986, Dangerfield had told MacIver that all Myshkowsky would take was accessory after the fact, which bears a maximum sentence of fourteen years. MacIver, a very experienced

Crown Attorney George Dangerfield (photo: The Winnipeg Sun)

Donald MacIver, Lee Colgan's lawyer (photo: Lisa Priest)

and talented lawyer, told Dangerfield to forget it – he'd call what he thought was a bluff and go through a preliminary hearing. He knew the Crown wouldn't make it to trial. "All they had on my client was third-class hearsay [evidence]," MacIver recalled.

MacIver knew that without Colgan, "Johnston would walk – they all would. The only way they could get a conviction was with my client." He also knew Colgan couldn't survive prison if he accepted only partial immunity because he would be regarded in the penitentiary as a "rat" and a Native-killer. (In maximum-security penitentiaries on the prairies, Natives make up more than 40 per cent of the inmates.)

Even though MacIver would never have admitted it to Dangerfield, he was tense and a little worried during the bargaining. "I felt the best defence was to never go to trial but he [Dangerfield] used every argument in the book," MacIver said later. "I didn't want to take even a very slight chance that Colgan would get convicted and I wanted to deal." But MacIver knew dealing on first-degree murder just wasn't done. "I can't remember a time it was done in the province. I don't think it has been," he remarked.

MacIver knew he had the best poker hand. Dangerfield then tried another tactic, telling MacIver that he had "new" evidence against Colgan that would put him in a maximum-security penitentiary for life. "Well, all right, George, you keep telling me that," MacIver recalled saying. "Why don't you give me a preview of this new evidence?" Dangerfield didn't; he must have known that MacIver had successfully called the bluff. Dangerfield grudgingly agreed to granting Colgan total immunity. He had lost.

Shortly afterwards, Colgan was told to think things over fast. As Colgan took a short walk outside the courthouse, he bumped into a couple of Johnston's friends who were trying to figure out why the preliminary hearing hadn't started yet.

"Hey, what's going on, Lee?" one of them asked a jittery Colgan. "I've got twenty minutes to decide what to do with the rest of my life," Colgan answered. Colgan told the pair that he had a choice: to blame the murder on Johnston or be stuck with serving a minimum of twenty-five years in prison, a sentence he said he couldn't cut. "Dwayne's tough and strong; he can handle prison – I can't," Colgan explained and later repeated a similar statement in court. Colgan must have known that Johnston would be "taken care of" by his biker buddies in prison. Johnston's friends tried to dissuade Colgan.

They were unsuccessful, however: Colgan decided to take the deal of immunity. And what a bargain it was. Not only did he get off of a charge of first-degree murder but he also would not be charged with sexual assault, unlawful confinement, kidnapping, and accessory after the fact – all criminal acts he had admitted to having committed the night of the killing. Under the Canada Evidence Act, Colgan would never be arrested for any of those charges, some of which carry a maximum sentence of life imprisonment.

The deal between the Attorney General's department and Lee Colgan read as follows:

I am instructed to tell you that in return for your client giving evidence in respect of the murder of Helen Betty Osborne on November 13, 1971, both at the Preliminary Hearing and subsequent trial of Dwayne Archie Johnston and James Paul Houghton for the murder of Helen Betty Osborne, that the charge of Murder in the First Degree will be withdrawn against Lee Scott Colgan and that no further proceedings will be taken against Lee Scott Colgan in relation to that charge of Murder, a charge of Rape or any other offence in any way related to the murder of Helen Betty Osborne, November 13, 1971. This undertaking by me as an agent of the Attorney General is given on the understanding that Lee Scott Colgan will give evidence to the best of his ability when called upon to do so, but does not depend on the outcome of the proceedings against James Paul Houghton and Dwayne Archie Johnston.

And then in your portion, Mr. Colgan:

I, Lee Scott Colgan, understand these terms set out above and agree to give evidence to the best of my ability according to them and any proceedings taken against James Paul Houghton and Dwayne Archie Johnston or either of them arising out of the murder of Helen Betty Osborne, November 13, 1971.

Around suppertime Colgan went back to his parents' home. His ex-wife Arlene Demmings had been invited to dinner. "It's all over," Lee said, breathing a sigh of relief. Lee was in the clear. Except now he had to wonder if Johnston's biker buddies were going to take revenge on him for "ratting out."

Five days later, Colgan had given the cops enough evidence to charge Jim Houghton, one of his closest friends for the past thirty years. "I think he felt badly about it," MacIver recalled. "Jim was a friend of his."

On March 15, 1987, Houghton had just dropped off his two sons at his house in Lethbridge and was returning to a friend's house when the cops nabbed him on the porch and arrested him for first-degree murder.

"He was like a ghost," friend Diane Alstad recalled. "But he seemed very calm." But Houghton's wife wasn't. "She [Shannon] got sick for maybe an hour or two but after that seemed to take it very well."

Alstad had no clue as to what had happened and asked Shannon what was going on. "She told me she didn't know and from her reaction I believed her. She was white and drained completely," Alstad recalled. "I talked to Shannon and she said: 'I can't believe this is happening – he's never raised his hand over me.' "

At first Shannon was reluctant to tell the children about the arrest. But after one of her boys saw a news report on television and starting asking questions, she had no choice. Shannon told them that there had been an accident a long time ago in which someone was killed. Their father had to go answer a few questions before the judge but would be home soon.

According to Alstad, the southern Alberta city of about 59,000 was in a state of shock following Houghton's arrest. No one could believe that Jim Houghton – the former hockey coach – had been charged with first-degree murder. "The RCMP very seldom make mistakes but when they charged Jim we were all wondering," Alstad, a former parole officer, recalled. "Everyone felt he hadn't been involved and even if he had been, he deserved a fair trial, anyway."

When it came time for his friends in Lethbridge to ask Houghton what this was all about, he replied that he had been in the car the night of the murder but had been let out at six or seven o'clock that evening – several hours before the killing.

Houghton's bail hearing was held in Winnipeg on March 24, 1987. Crown Attorney George Dangerfield asked that Justice Vern Simonsen release Houghton under only the strictest terms. "It was a vicious killing, a senseless killing and one which, if convicted, would put Mr. Houghton in prison for the balance of his life," Dangerfield said in court. But Dangerfield added, "There are things in his favour. He is a married man, has his own home, has a job and it might not be in the public interest to take all that away from him."

As Houghton did not have a criminal record and had lead a seemingly model life, he was released for $30,000 and a $100,000 surety his mother, Margaret Helen Houghton, put up based on two properties with a clear title she had had estimated. As well, he was required to report once a week to the RCMP in Lethbridge.

Houghton's employer, Hilti, guaranteed him a job unless he was convicted; Johnston's employer, CP Rail, also held his job open, not thinking he would ever be convicted of the murder. One of Johnston's superiors, who strongly believed in his innocence, even offered to testify at his trial.

Later, Lee Colgan would travel from The Pas to Winnipeg to meet behind closed doors with Houghton's lawyer, John Scurfield, an extremely bright and highly reputable lawyer. Defence lawyers don't usually interview witnesses who are testifying for the prosecution because it could backfire on them. For instance, the witness could very well say at the trial, ''I know we talked about this earlier but no matter how many times you try to change my mind, I won't,'' and the lawyer, of course, would create the impression that he'd tried to manipulate the witness.

But it was Colgan who sought out Scurfield in September 1987, two months before the trial date. Lee Colgan asked his friend, Jack Halliday, to drive him to Winnipeg so he could talk to Houghton's lawyer. ''He phoned me one night and told me he wanted to go down there and see him [Scurfield] and he asked me if I'd drive him and I told him, 'No, I didn't want to,' and he phoned me back and I said, 'Ya, I'd take him' . . . It was definitely Lee who wanted to see him.'' Halliday didn't attend the meeting, but when Colgan tried to discuss it on the drive home, Halliday didn't want to hear about it. ''I didn't want to know,'' he said.

Why was Colgan, who had made a deal of immunity with the Crown, meeting with the lawyer of the man he was going to give evidence against? Was Colgan so wracked with guilt that he wanted to turn around and help his friend Houghton? Did Colgan just want to tell Scurfield what his evidence was? Or was he simply down in Winnipeg for a pleasant chat? Colgan won't talk about his reasons, and, while Scurfield doesn't deny the meeting took place, he refuses to comment on it.

One of Johnston's friends who heard about the meeting went to Scurfield's office in Winnipeg and asked him if

Colgan was framing Johnston for the killing. Scurfield said nothing and ushered Johnston's friend out of the office.

But whether Colgan helped or hindered Houghton is something Shannon Houghton is still trying to come to grips with. "Sometimes I imagine I'm walking down the street and I see Lee. I'd probably still talk to him because he's an alcoholic and a weaker person and they [police] took advantage of that," Shannon said. "But I still think I don't hate him and I honestly think Jim doesn't either . . . I don't know why they [police] just didn't leave these guys alone."

PART THREE

Justice on Trial

CHAPTER TWELVE

Senior Crown Attorney George Dangerfield opened the prosecution's case on Tuesday, November 24, 1987, shortly after 10:30 A.M.

Defence counsel and the prosecution had devoted the entire previous day to selecting the jury by testing potential jurors for their bias regarding the case. Both sides questioned potential jurors to see if they show any prejudice: perhaps they have previous knowledge of the case or have shown perceived discrimination towards Natives or whites.

Twenty Natives had been eliminated from the one hundred and four jury prospects, including one man who stood up in protest as he saw Natives being rejected from the panel and accused the defence counsel of being racist. "There was no deliberate campaign to keep the Natives off," lawyer John Scurfield said afterwards. "But we didn't want these men to be convicted for all of the ills of society." During jury selection, defence lawyers used thirty-nine of their forty possible rejections and ended up with an all-white two-woman, ten-man jury.

Defence counsel obviously wanted jurors who would be sympathetic to their clients' case – that's standard practice. But what better choice could be made than the white, working-class men who far outnumbered the two women on the panel? The men included a labourer, a plumber, an electrician, a first-aid attendant, a portsman, a branch manager, two supervisors, and two retirees. One woman was a florist, the other a homemaker. Only three jurors were from The Pas, the rest from surrounding areas such as Flin Flon and Swan River.

At one point, Dangerfield tried to have Johnston's biker friend, Wilf Cudmore, removed from the courtroom because he thought he was coaching Johnston's lawyer, in his selection of potential jurors.

Brodsky had already tried without success to move the trial from The Pas, presumably because he felt Johnston wouldn't get a fair hearing from a jury that had heard gossip about the case for sixteen years. He was also concerned that some townspeople on the jury may have believed that it was their responsibility to protect the town, which was as much on trial as the two accused. Even though Brodsky supported his request with a petition of twenty names Cudmore had rounded up, it was denied.

In the tiny courtroom, Dangerfield opened the Crown's case. At fifty-five, Dangerfield is one of the top prosecutors in Manitoba. He has managed over the years to impress judges with his authoritative style, decisiveness, and astuteness, even though he tends to seem self-absorbed both in and out of court. He told the twelve jurors that Dwayne Archie Johnston and James Robert Paul Houghton could be convicted of first-degree murder if the jury was satisfied beyond a reasonable doubt that the men had killed Helen Betty Osborne to escape responsibility for sexually assaulting and beating her. He also instructed the jury that they could find Houghton and Johnston guilty if they killed Osborne – even if by accident – during an attempted sexual assault.

Dangerfield said the Crown would be calling two witnesses – Lee Scott Colgan and Norman Bernard Manger – men who had been accomplices to the killing of Osborne. He also told the jurors not to blindly accept their testimony, as they had sat in the car while Betty Osborne was being stabbed to death just a few feet away. He added that the jurors should not be swayed by the fact that neither man would face criminal charges. The jurors should consider evidence other than the men's testimony.

Reading authoritatively from his notes, the six-foot, three-inch bespectacled prosecutor told the jury that Colgan, Manger, Johnston, and Houghton had been cruising the streets of The Pas looking for a compliant Native girl to have sex with on Friday, November 12, 1971. They hoped that Osborne, whom they had spotted walking along Third Street near Edwards Avenue, would be that girl.

Johnston had yanked the girl off of the street and pulled her into the car. When she refused to drink and resisted his sexual advances he had swung at her and torn at her clothes. It was Houghton, Dangerfield said, who had driven the men and girl out to the secluded cabin. There Johnston had tried to force her to be more compliant. When she wouldn't, he began beating her and ripping at her clothing.

Osborne's screams of terror had been so shrill and loud that the four decided to take her to an even more remote area in the wilderness – the pumphouse – where Johnston had dragged her out of the car once again. The sounds of Betty being smacked and banged against the trunk had been so loud and rocked the car so fiercely that Colgan asked Houghton, the biggest of the four, to go help the girl.

After Houghton got out of the car, Johnston came back to the vehicle and reached under the seat for a screwdriver. Afterwards, Colgan didn't hear a sound. He said the three had only been outside for a few minutes when he jumped into the front seat, turned the car around, shone the headlights into the bush but saw nothing. That's when he stuck his head outside the window and yelled, "I'm leaving," a couple of times. At least one of the men yelled back, "Just a minute."

Johnston and Houghton then jumped into the back seat and Colgan sped away down icy Highway 10 back to town, leaving Betty Osborne for dead in the bush. Colgan wasn't sure if they had gone back to the Houghton cabin before returning to town. On the trip home Colgan had asked where the girl was and someone in the back seat had replied, "She's dead."

"Now the prosecution's case then," Dangerfield told the jurors, sitting stiffly in their seats, "is simply this: that what began as a party with sex if it were available ended in murder because these two men, Houghton and Johnston, realized when they were at the pumphouse that they'd gone too far and there was nothing left but to kill."

Dangerfield's address took a little more than half an hour. While he was speaking, Justine Osborne and her daughter Cecilia sat weeping in the front row of the courtroom, reliving dreadful memories of the murder. Betty's family, who had been waiting patiently to hear the truth for sixteen years, had no idea the murder had involved four men, two of whom, at least, would escape scot-free. The revelation soured Justine towards the trial from the very beginning.

Immediately after his opening address, Dangerfield began calling his witnesses. With the help of Assistant Crown Attorney Daniel Dutchin he called his first witness, Kenneth Gurba, who told the jury that he had stumbled onto the mutilated, naked body of Osborne while hunting for rabbit tracks at the age of fourteen. "It looked like it was nude except for a pair of, possibly a pair of shoes. And the face looked very bloody," he testified. He and his father had run across the road to the flight services desk of The Pas airport and asked the worker there to call for an RCMP officer. The worker replied that an RCMP officer had just landed. They then had told him the story and gone back to the scene where they had remained until police finished photographing the tire tracks. It had been an awful experience.

The Crown's second witness was Don Knight, the chief investigating officer in 1971. The forty-year-old man was now a lawyer, dressed impeccably in a navy blue pin-stripe suit. Now he was defending men he would have scraped off the streets to arrest sixteen years earlier.

Dutchin had Knight introduce almost all of the forty-two pieces of evidence, the first being a book of ten colour photographs, two of which depicated the savagely murdered girl. Four books of pictures were passed around to the jurors, who sat huddled in groups of three, looking at colour pictures of the car that had transported Osborne to her death; the blood-stained heel marks the killers had left in the snow; the supposed murder weapon, and other shots.

It wasn't until jurors flipped to the third page that they saw the shocking sight of Betty Osborne's bloodied body lying nude in the snow. Her left arm was bent, her right index finger pointing to her heart, and her legs, bearing her high, black rubber boots, were crossed. Blood was smeared in streams up and down her stomach and her face was mutilated. The photograph prompted several jurors to look straight across to the prisoner's dock at a blank-faced Houghton and Johnston. Some jurors looked at them with disgust, others with fury. The pictures had had the desired effect.

Other pieces of sixteen-year-old evidence including pill bottles containing dried blood; Betty's soiled clothing; hair from her head, abdomen, and pubic area; two screwdrivers and the notebook paper from which Osborne's fingerprint had been lifted to indentify her body.

But there would be no footprint casts admitted into evidence and only one photograph of two imprints that looked like shoes with pointed toes. Later, the defence would attempt to tear a hole in the prosecution's case because the identification officer at the scene, Harold Bielert, had not made casts of any of the footprints, nor had he made any record in his now sixteen-year-old notes of the two sets of footprints leading up to the body, as constable Don Knight had done. Knight had noticed a set of footprints on each side of the body, but they had been made in softer snow and were less distinct than the other footprints found in the parking lot.

Sometimes, footprint casts can be as useful as fingerprints when identifying murder suspects, but usually only when there are strangely similar characteristics, such as a worn-down part of a shoe. Even then a cast is usually made from a distinct impression. Footprint casts can create a strong suspicion regarding one suspect or raise serious doubts about others. Bielert, now a real estate salesman, said quite simply that no one had asked him to take casts so he hadn't done so.

He hadn't taken photographs of the tire treads, either, which might have shown where the car had stopped, how many people had gotten out, whether they had gotten out or been pushed out, and what kind of shoes they had been wearing, Brodsky said. Later, police said they hadn't taken such casts because the prints weren't distinct enough and the procedure would have melted what little impression had been made in the snow.

The trial was promising to be one of the hottest news stories the province had experienced for years. Manitobans had seen their share of bizarre murder trials, but nothing with this much intrigue. The case reeked of the racial tensions witnessed in the southern United States in the 1960s, but these were now surfacing in Canada in 1987. It appeared that perhaps the Native woman's death hadn't been vigorously investigated because she had been living in a horribly racist town.

It wasn't until Lee Colgan took the stand half-way through the trial that the real story came to life: a story of drugs, boozing, and sixteen years of nightmares related by a man who couldn't live with the murder, who had constantly talked about it to friends, neighbours, strangers – anyone who would listen. It was a tale about a town that had protected him and his three cohorts from prosecution by not going to police with murder confessions that had been blurted out numerous times over the years.

As Colgan had spilled out his story in the past, usually

while on LSD, MDA, or his eighth glass of beer, it was rarely the same twice. But he remembered the sound of Betty Osborne being smashed against the back fender of his father's car and her shrill screams for help. And he couldn't escape the thought of her dying moments, alone, bleeding to death, naked and freezing in the bush while he sped the killers to safety in the get-away car.

Never would Colgan be able to banish these nightmares from his mind; they preyed upon him, ate at his soul. No matter how much he wracked his body and mind with booze and drugs, he couldn't erase that unforgettable night, the night he'd been an accomplice to murder.

Visibly shaken, Colgan described a life of torment by the police in which he was sent screwdriver drinks as the cops constantly tried to provoke a murder confession from him. He said police never let up; each year they visited him, trying to get him to speak about the killing. "When my children were born they were there hours after because they knew I'd be drunk celebrating," Colgan said. "It's times like that that I wouldn't talk to them 'cause I knew what they wanted."

As quiet as he was with the police, however, he was loose-lipped with townfolk. "Within a week or two weeks after it happened, it was quite common knowledge around town that the four of us were involved," Colgan said. He couldn't recall on the stand how many people in town he'd told.

It was at that moment that the town also went on trial. The Pas residents were in a prisoner's dock of their own. But some of them were also seated in the jury box and the eyes of the nation's press were scrutinizing them. What really made the press explode was the conspiracy of silence among the townspeople. It had included the local sheriff, who also had heard a murder confession.

Newspapers across the country picked the story up, as did *Maclean's* magazine, Alberta's *Western Report*, *The Globe and Mail* and CBC's *fifth estate*, where it gained national prominence. *Saturday Night* also decided to do an article on it. An American magazine called *Inside Detective* also did a lengthy feature on the case.

Ironically, the trial made the front page of the bi-weekly *Opasquia Times* in The Pas, but certain facts, such as the sheriff hearing a murder confession, were carefully buried inside the paper. The freelance reporter who covered the story said the higher-ups wouldn't have it any other way.

The townspeople's defensiveness regarding the trial was instant. Johnston's friend, Cudmore, ripped the camera out of one freelance photographer's hands outside the courthouse and exposed the film. The freelancer refused to take pictures of witnesses leaving court after that incident, fearing he would be beaten up.

Soon the murder was gaining as much prominence as the infamous case of Donald Marshall, who served eleven years in a Nova Scotia prison for a murder he didn't commit. Marshall was convicted the same year The Pas residents began looking the other way when talk of the Native girl's killers surfaced. They were both ugly cases of terrible injustice.

And that's what kept running through the minds of the Native people, whose presence grew as the trial continued. Just a few days after the trial began, the Natives from the nearby The Pas Reserve started lining up to wait for one of the fifty courtroom seats, while others stood against the back courtroom walls waiting to hear all the details.

Before the fourth man, Norm Manger, took the stand, Brian Johnson told the court that he had been in the Colgan car hours before the killing. Johnson, seventeen at the time of the killing, said he and a man named Gordon Buck had been picked up by Colgan, Houghton, and Norm Manger on November 12, 1971. Colgan had been driving so badly, and the car was fishtailing so often, that he had gotten out and begun walking. Shortly afterwards, Johnson said they had picked him up again, except this time Jim Houghton was driving. He couldn't remember much about the night, except that when he got out of the car Houghton was still driving. He didn't remember Dwayne Johnston ever being in the car.

The testimony that many spectators waited for was that of Norm Manger. It was a missing piece of the puzzle. Apparently he hadn't discussed the killing, but had managed to live with it somehow.

It was especially difficult for old friends to hear the testimony of Manger, who appeared burnt out after so many years of drinking. His appearance was equally puzzling to Natives because he looked so much like one of them yet had been involved in the killing.

On the stand Manger, pale and shaking, told the jury he had given phoney alibis to police over the years because he had wanted to escape punishment for being at the scene of the crime. "I knew I didn't do anything, so I just didn't want to do anything to just, like, wanted to say I just wasn't there period," Manger said. Hiding under a mop of black hair, he looked down at the floor during his testimony. The only thing he remembered from that night was getting into a car after attending a dance. The next thing he knew he was glancing out the window at what he thought was a snow drift when he saw someone being dragged. And he was terrified.

His memory fogged from alcohol, Manger said he had grabbed his head, crawled under the dashboard of the car, and began whimpering like a baby. The self-described alcoholic said he woke up the next day – he can't remember where – trying to figure out what had happened the night before. "I guess I started drinking again and then I bumped into one of the people mentioned there, and I don't remember who it was and kind of found out what I guess that did happen the night before." Shortly after the killing, Manger said, he had talked with Johnston and Houghton at separate times and they had agreed once again to keep the murder quiet.

Only two weeks before the trial had he finally told police what he knew. We don't know how chief investigating officer Bob Urbanoski managed to convince Manger into testifying for the Crown but his visits to Cranbrook must have been very persuasive. It was a good thing for the prosecution that he did testify. Had Manger, the fourth man, not been there to testify, the defence would have ripped a hole through the Crown's case, simply by asking where the fourth man was and what he had done. Perhaps he had been the killer, they could say.

The most damning evidence about Johnston was skilfully placed just after Colgan's testimony. Andrea Wiwcharuk took the stand. The stout brunette told a hushed courtroom she remembered Dwayne Johnston saying at a trailer camp party in the winter of 1972, ''I picked up a screwdriver and I stabbed her and I stabbed her and I stabbed her.'' Wiwcharuk, fourteen at the time of the party, said Johnston had made those comments as he stood up and made stabbing motions with his hands until his girlfriend, Arlee White, told him to be quiet. All eyes in the courtroom turned to Johnston, who rolled his eyes and shook his head in apparent disbelief. To onlookers, he appeared to be bragging about the killing. But to this day he maintains he never made those comments, as does Manger, who was also supposed to be there.

Shortly after that episode, Wiwcharuk said, Johnston claimed, ''They tore the car apart and we'll never get caught.'' A few guests, including Norman Manger, had laughed. Either Rick or Lee Colgan had laughed as well – she wasn't sure which one was at the party. Johnston had apparently sat back down and boasted to one of the party guests: ''Do you know what it feels like to kill someone? It feels great.'' That may have been all the jury needed to hear.

One of Johnston's problems in court was his tendency to project his fear and guilt. During the trial, regardless of what he was really feeling, Johnston looked guilty when Wiwcharuk gave her testimony, smug when his lawyer skilfully examined the police's physical evidence, and angry as Colgan took the stand.

Houghton, on the other hand, masked whatever anxieties

he seemed to be feeling, and appeared relaxed throughout most of the trial. He even jotted down notes regularly, presumably to bring up details with his lawyer at recess. If Houghton felt any guilt at all for what he'd done, no one would have known it.

One person who wanted answers about the night of the killing was Isaiah Osborne, now thirty-four. Coincidentally, he was on a remand at The Pas jail for stealing thirty-three dollars and punching a man out at a party. He occupied a cell not far from Dwayne Johnston's. He often saw Jim Houghton going into the consulting room. "I almost talked to him," Isaiah recalled of Johnston. "I just wanted to ask him what he did to my sister so that I would know, but I decided to forget it."

The last of the Crown's twenty-three witnesses, Dr. Donald Penner, detailed clinically the horrifying wounds Betty Osborne had suffered. The elderly forensic pathologist with fifty years' experience said that there had been contusion to the lungs, meaning that small blood vessels had burst and bled into the tissues – an injury likely made with a fist, or by kneeling or jumping on chest. As well, her right kidney was torn and bleeding. Eleven of the fifty-odd stab wounds were to her chest and nipple area, others to her back, including one 5.5-centimetres-deep stab wound to the back of the head, penetrating the brain. Still others were to her head and face, some so close together that, because her skin was so torn, he couldn't tell how many there were.

Penner said the bloodied screwdriver seized near the scene could have made all the wounds except one. He said it was very unlikely that the screwdriver Colgan identified as the murder weapon could have made the 5.5-centimetre gash that cracked her skull. To do such a thing, the brain and the skull would have had to have been in such a position as to permit the maximum length of that blade to penetrate the head. He said it would be more likely that the second screwdriver found near the highway had made that deep gash.

As well, her left ear had been cut about five centimetres,

almost ripped off. Osborne had died from shock and haemmorhaging due to multiple head injuries, he concluded. He couldn't be certain if Betty Osborne had still been alive when the men had left her in the bush but said it was a possibility because the snow had melted under her body, causing an imprint in the snow.

On that note, the prosecution's case was put to rest.

CHAPTER THIRTEEN

They were two defence lawyers trying desperately to get their clients off first-degree murder charges. And their plans of attack were as radically different as the men they represented.

There was friendly, smiling John Scurfield, with his boyish looks and country-boy charm. He projected himself as a down-home boy, just trying to do his job the best he could. He referred to his client, Jim Houghton, countless times as "a nice guy," model citizen, family man — hardly a person capable of such a vicious crime. "My client was truly an individual you could empathize with," Scurfield said later.

Greg Brodsky, the top criminal lawyer representing Dwayne Johnston, projected himself as being hard-nosed, sarcastic, and cool. His defence consisted of telling the jury that they couldn't rely on the testimony of a bought witness with so much to gain – that of Lee Scott Colgan. Brodsky argued that Colgan's word couldn't be trusted because he was an admitted chronic alcoholic who had told many versions of the killing while trying to banish a sixteen-year nightmare with anything he could drink and any pill he could pop. "He [Colgan] sold his soul to put that man [Johnston] in jail," he said.

Despite their different styles, both lawyers tried to find a way to get their clients freed. And they began by cross-examining every piece of physical evidence collected by the police until it seemed to be no more than a mishmash of vague recollections.

Scurfield zoomed in on the first witness, Kenneth Gurba, who had found the naked corpse. Gurba wore about a size-11 shoe at the time. Scurfield suggested that maybe the boy, then about six feet, had made the footprints leading up to the body rather than his client, Houghton. In his insistent, overly polite manner he tried desperately to establish the possibility – no matter how remote – that Gurba could have made one set of tracks while walking up to the body. Gurba didn't agree.

Throughout the trial, it was crucial that Scurfield try to reveal through cross-examination that those footprints could have been left by someone else or that there was some doubt as to their existence. He went through just about every witness trying to evoke this possibility. It was also crucial that the fresh-faced, fair-haired lawyer appear to be a nice guy by impressing the jury of good, common folk with his upstanding morality and friendly, polite disposition.

As a youngster, Scurfield had attended trials in rural Manitoba towns with his father, also a lawyer. There he had developed his passion for criminal law. Scurfield, by his own admission, loves the drama of the courtroom. He was given the best actor award in his high-school theatre group, and this talent has come in handy during his performances in criminal law cases.

At the age of thirty-six, the married father of three is already considered one of the province's finest criminal lawyers. He is considered by the legal community to be very confident, aggressive, extremely bright, and conscientious. He is fast on his feet, and reputed to be a tough scrapper on behalf of his clients. He is a consistently strong cross-examiner and is good at impressing some judges in court.

In this case, Scurfield had to cope with some tough evidence: refuting that two men had gotten out of the car and that two men had dragged Osborne's body to its final resting spot. Assuming Johnston was one of them, the Crown's implication was that Houghton must have been the other.

Two screwdrivers had been presented in court – the implication being that Houghton must have used the second one to help kill Betty Osborne. Scurfield, however, had an astute explanation for the presence of the second screwdriver. He told the jury that as the four men drove away from the murder scene, they had panicked, blindly throwing anything they found on the car floor out the windows. That included a second screwdriver that hadn't even been involved in the killing, he said.

One last possibility was to believe what Colgan had told his lawyer Don MacIver: the real murder weapon had been thrown deep into the bush and the police had never recovered it. According to MacIver, Colgan had said he had no idea where the second screwdriver had come from. In court, however, Colgan identified the screwdriver found by the side of the road as the murder weapon.

Scurfield's strategy was to try to convince the jury that his client, Houghton, had only tried to control the maniacal Johnston, who flipped out and killed poor Betty Osborne. But by the time Houghton had gotten out of the car or just shortly after, which would have been too late, Osborne had suffered fifty stab wounds and was dead.

It wasn't until the second witness, Don Knight, took the stand that Scurfield's two theories about how both sets of footprints got on either side of the dragged body were tested. (Knight had been the chief investigating officer at the time of the murder.)

Scurfield's first theory was that the Mounties, Ken Gurba, or perhaps the other fisherman at the lake could have made one set of footprints leading up to the body. Since the police hadn't distinguished the killer's footprints from the others in their notes, Scurfield suggested that Gurba or the others could have made them while taking a look at the body. Knight didn't agree. "There's the marks on the side which means they have to have at least one arm. If they had the other arm the drag marks would be, would not be heel drag marks but would be either flat feet or there'd been an arm drag or there'd be some other markings rather than just the one, so it had to be two," Knight said on the witness stand.

Scurfield's second theory, seemingly less plausible, was that one person could have dragged the body by both arms, and that the drag marks could have obliterated the killer's footprints. Two people could then have walked into the scene, creating two sets of footprints leading up to the body. Knight agreed that was a possibility. "But then you have to explain how they get out of there," he added. The second theory didn't work either.

But it wasn't until both lawyers, one after the other, challenged Knight that the police work at the scene appeared questionable. Knight had assisted corporal Harold Bielert in taking footprint measurements.

The lawyers each vigorously went after both officers for not taking casts of the footprints or any other marks in the snow – something it was suggested they should have done. Brodsky further asked Bielert why he hadn't taken casts or photographs of the tire tracks near the pumphouse, especially since police had instructed Gurba not to leave because they had wanted to do exactly that. Brodsky argued that such photographs could have helped indicate how many people exited the car, whether they were pushed out or walked out, and if the car had sped away.

Footprint casts can help to determine the guilt or innocence of suspects, but usually only when there is a very good impression left, one that could show characteristics such as foot size, or wear and tear to a particular shoe. Sometimes, when compared to the size of an accused's foot, they can also eliminate a suspect by showing that his feet were likely too large or small to make those impressions.

John Scurfield, Jim Houghton's lawyer (photo: Lisa Priest)

Greg Brodsky, Dwayne Johnston's lawyer
(photo: The Winnipeg Sun)

For instance, Dwayne Johnston wears a size 8 to 8 1/2 shoe, yet the three distinct sets of footprints at the scene were 11 1/2, 12, and 12 1/2 inches long and were most likely made by about a size-10 shoe, corporal Harold Bielert had said. A size 8 1/2 medium-soled shoe is about 10 1/2 inches long, and unlikely to make an impression of 11 1/2 inches. However, a size 8 1/2 boot could make an 11 1/2-inch impression.

While it could have been argued by the Crown that Johnston had been wearing big biker boots that had made those impressions, Brodsky could have argued quite accurately that, from the point of view of size alone, it was more likely that the feet of Houghton, Colgan, or Manger had made those prints. Such a tactic could have raised a doubt in the minds of the jurors. Brodsky said later he had considered bringing up the discrepancy in the footprints at the trial but he didn't because that would have meant calling Johnston as a witness. He could have also requested that a jail guard measure Johnston's feet in court – the judge might have consented – presented that measurement to the jury, and cross-examined Bielert about it. In any event, he chose not to make Johnston's footprint size an issue.

Of the two defence lawyers, Brodsky had the tougher case. It was nearly impossible to get an acquittal. After all, the Crown had Colgan's testimony blaming Johnston for killing Osborne as well as that of Andrea Wiwcharuk. Tremendous pressure was put on the jury to get a conviction – the town was on trial as much as Johnston and someone had to pay. Besides, Scurfield, Houghton's lawyer, was pointing the finger at Johnston at every legally available opportunity. Scurfield was becoming Brodsky's biggest stumbling block.

It's no wonder that Johnston had picked Brodsky for a lawyer. As one of the province's highest-profile criminal lawyers, he has acted on about 260 murder cases – usually the most notorious – over his twenty-nine-year career. Canada's most famous criminal lawyer, Toronto's

Eddie Greenspan, thinks so highly of Brodsky that he refers cases to him on a regular basis, and gets referrals in return. "I work twenty hours a day and I'm sure Greg works more," Greenspan has commented. Brodsky's eldest son, thirty-year-old Daniel, is articling with Greenspan's Toronto firm. Another Winnipeg lawyer has described Brodsky as "probably the hardest-working character I've ever met."

Brodsky is regarded as one of the best criminal lawyers in Manitoba. Some members of the legal community dispute this, claiming he's a plodder, who lacks courtroom charisma and who has built his career by taking on too many cases at once and being a media hound. "Greg can smell a microphone fifteen feet away," said one lawyer.

Despite those criticisms, Brodsky, an incredibly blunt man, has a public reputation as a great lawyer and a fighter. He is one of the most relentless and methodical researchers in the business. Included among his most famous clients is Henry Morgentaler. He also defended Thomas Sophonow, twice convicted but ultimately acquitted of murdering a sixteen-year-old doughnut-shop waitress named Barbara Stoppel. At forty-eight, he juggles as many as sixteen murder cases at once, sleeps an average of just four hours a night, and jogs exactly sixty-two miles a week. Somehow he still manages to spend time with his family.

Brodsky's defence of Johnston consisted of ripping apart police evidence and trying to convince the jury that they could not rely on Colgan's testimony because he had too much to gain by testifying. He hammered away at Bielert for not taking photographs of the tire tracks and suggested that it was important physical evidence that had been overlooked at the scene.

"I did not see any tire marks in the vicinity of the pumphouse that were suitable for taking photographs of or casts of," Bielert said in court. "To the best of my knowledge, there weren't any tire tracks there to be photographed.'' Bielert also testified he had taken photographs of the ten sets of footprints but he didn't know where the pictures were now. All he was aware of were the pictures entered into evidence. To the best of his knowledge, he said, he couldn't remember even having the facilities to make footprint casts in 1971.

One puzzling piece of evidence was the warrant to search Colgan's car, executed seven months after the murder. While the information on the warrant was not read out in court, it had said that the 1967 Chrysler sedan had been seen in the immediate area of Clearwater Lake at the time of the murder. Colgan, Norman Manger, and James Houghton had been together on the night, and that the three ''might reasonably be involved in the commission of the crime.'' Incredibly, the warrant did not mention Johnston, the prime suspect.

John Fitzmaurice, the RCMP corporal stationed in Dauphin, Manitoba, who had obtained the search warrant on June 20, 1972, said under cross-examination by Brodsky that Johnston hadn't been named in the warrant because he simply wasn't a suspect in the murder.

Later, out of court, there were suggestions that the brassière strap and clasp were planted in the car by police, who were desperate to produce substantial evidence to nail the four men after waiting so long to look for it.

But the first real blow to the prosecution's case against Houghton didn't come until Bielert said he had nothing in his sixteen-year-old notes about two sets of footprints on either side of the drag marks, which would suggest that two people had lugged Osborne's body into the bush. Through cross-examination, Scurfield skilfully poked a hole in the prosecution's case and let it rest that Bielert, the man in charge of evidence, didn't have any information about two sets of footprints in his notes because there hadn't been two sets in the first place. Scurfield suggested that Johnston alone had dragged the body deep into the bush.

Minutes later, after the judge asked the jury to leave

(a situation called a voir dire), Bielert told Mr. Justice Sidney Schwartz that he had made a mistake. He said he remembered there being two sets of footprints after all, and he wanted to have the chance to correct his mistake. Naturally, Scurfield didn't want him to but the judge insisted Bielert correct himself, saying it was in the interests of justice. Even though Bielert corrected himself, Scurfield asked him if perhaps he had recalled the drag marks after discussing the topic with Knight. Bielert disagreed. But it was clear that his failure to remember that crucial information from the outset had hurt the prosecution's case.

All told, both Brodsky and Scurfield revealed major inconsistencies in the police work – their delay in obtaining the search warrant, their failure to take footprint casts and to distinguish the killer's footprints from those made by Gurba and the air forces officer, and finally the evidence that Johnston hadn't even been a suspect seven months after the killing. Brodsky also suggested that Bielert could have gotten a better camera lens, which would have provided better pictures of footprints, had he simply taken the time to ride into town and pick one up from a store. Bielert agreed. Those inconsistencies immediately confirmed the public's suspicion that the police hadn't investigated Osborne's death thoroughly – perhaps because she was Native. It reeked of laziness.

Scurfield managed to get the fourth man, Norm Manger, who remembered very little about the killing, to testify that he remembered Jim Houghton telling him he hadn't killed the girl.

But the most challenging moments for both lawyers came when Lee Colgan took the stand. After the prosecution questioned Colgan, he remained on the witness stand so the defence could cross-examine him. This was their opportunity to break the main link in a long chain of circumstantial evidence. Colgan spilled out the gruesome murder in vivid detail. Everyone had been anxiously awaiting his testimony thinking that finally, after sixteen years, they would hear the awful truth about what really had happened that night.

Visibly shaken and wide-eyed, Colgan testified under cross-examination that he had helped sexually assault and beat Betty Osborne. He expanded on that when Brodsky, counsel for Johnston, referred to a statement Colgan had made to police on March 10, 1987. Police had asked Colgan if he, Manger, and Houghton had helped Johnston in his struggle with the girl at Houghton's cabin.

> Colgan: I did. She was fighting with him and Dwayne sort of had some of her clothes off. I knew she wasn't going to do anything. Dwayne and I put her back in the car. I think some of her clothes were left behind, her top or something or half of her bra. I'm not exactly sure.

At first Brodsky's cross-examination of Colgan seemed clumsy and his questions awkwardly worded. Several times Colgan asked Brodsky to repeat himself, saying he didn't understand the question. However, Brodsky soon became more articulate. Brodsky hammered away at Colgan, each time bringing out more and more details of his involvement. Colgan was being dragged more deeply into the killing, and it seemed as if he had a substantially larger role in it than he wanted to admit. Brodsky was gaining ground on exposing Colgan as a self-serving weasel.

Over and over again Brodsky went at him until finally Colgan seemed to be completely confused about how to answer. The whole courtroom went into a state of shock when Colgan, in a moment of weakness, finally admitted that he'd pointed the finger at Johnston just to get off a first-degree murder charge. What some townspeople had suspected all along had finally become fact. The public was in awe.

> Brodsky: . . . that's the reason you pointed the finger

at Dwayne Archie Johnston, because you had to point
it at somebody. You had to sell something. Isn't that
right?

Colgan: Yes, I suppose.

Brodsky: So whether he did it or not was irrelevant.
You couldn't do the time. You had an alcohol problem,
you had a sick father, you didn't want to go to jail.
Anyways he wasn't around, that is, he was out of town,
so you were going to point the finger at him. Isn't that
what happened?

Colgan: Yeah, that's right.

But Colgan's tale didn't stop there. He admitted under
Brodsky's cross-examination that no matter what way he
"wiggled and turned," he wasn't going to get off a
murder charge unless he blamed Johnston. So why
shouldn't he? Colgan said he couldn't go to jail – it would
kill his father – he couldn't let that happen.

To discredit him even more, Brodsky also brought up
several versions of the killing he'd told other people over
the years, including one he told a local girl from The
Pas, Annette Veito. She was also the girl who had seen
a figure walking down the street the night of the murder
before being picked up in the Colgan car. Police believed
that figure was Betty Osborne. Colgan denied telling
Veito on December 1, 1984, that, "We had her [Osborne]
stripped by the time we got to the airport. I was driving
the car and Norman was passed out in the back." But
Brodsky used that statement in an attempt to show that
Colgan was either lying or mistaken when he had testified
earlier that Houghton had been driving and that Betty
Osborne still had on some clothes by the time they got
to the pumphouse.

Brodsky also suggested that Colgan had told his friend
Jack Halliday on an earlier occasion that he had been too
drunk to really remember what happened during the killing. Halliday apparently had told Colgan it wasn't even
his apartment that the men had broken into that night –

it was someone else's. Colgan had believed it was because that's what Houghton had told him. And he had the type of wine wrong – it wasn't Red Devil.

In an effort to further break down his credibility, Brodsky accused Colgan of telling sheriff Gerald Wilson about the killing in yet another effort to bargain for his immunity. Brodsky suggested that Colgan was trying to get the sheriff to pull some strings for him in the summer of 1977 or 1978 when he related the tale of the murder in his camper truck after having a couple of drinks at the Royal Canadian Legion.

Colgan had been drinking with Wilson when a vodka screwdriver arrived at the table, courtesy of the RCMP. The tactic worked, except that the RCMP expected the sheriff to report the murder confession immediately – not eight or nine years later. The delay cost Wilson a demotion, a $2,500-a-year pay cut, and a transfer to another town. Vic Schroeder, then Attorney General, said he would have fired Wilson if he could have made it stick with the civil service commission and described the sheriff's behaviour as inexcusable.

A letter from Deputy Attorney General Tanner Elton explained Wilson's demotion this way: "Had you properly and expediently brought this information to the RCMP in such a way to make the significance of the information clearly known, this information would have had a substantive influence on the expediency of the investigating process." Wilson recently won his grievance and has been reinstated as sheriff with back pay. Arbitrator Martin Freedman ruled that the penalty was inappropriate and ordered that Wilson be given a twenty-one-day suspension without pay. Ron Cann, labour relations officer with the provincial civil service commission, said: "Unfortunately, there was no legal obligation for him to report a murder confession. But we felt there was a breach of trust in the court system."

The Manitoba Government Employees Association argued that Wilson told an RCMP officer "in passing" about the conversation but didn't write out a formal police statement. As there was no legal obligation to report the murder confession, the Commission had to prove that Wilson didn't do his job, Wilson has refused to comment. Even though in Canada sheriffs are not law enforcers, as they are in United States, they have an obligation, at least a moral one, to report such a confession. The role of the sheriff, as an officer of the court, is to deliver subpoenas and to transport prisoners in many towns. The sheriff, the most senior local staff member, is also an administrator.

When Brodsky asked Colgan why he had spoken with Wilson, Colgan replied, "He was a friend of mine."

By now, the murder case had taken on the plot of a prime-time television show. It had all of the elements: the silent town, the grossly obese, eccentric lawyer who'd acted for all four, and the sheriff who heard a murder confession but did nothing about it. People in the court-room were hanging off the edges of their seats waiting to hear what other sordid surprises awaited them in cross-examination. People who had no connection to the vic-tim, the accused, or even the town crammed into the back of the courtroom. Some were turned away because of lack of seats.

Brodsky referred to one of Colgan's earlier police state-ments on April 20, 1987, in which he'd talked about telling sheriff Wilson about the murder:

RCMP: Do you remember talking to Gerald Wilson about the murder?
Colgan: Yeah.
RCMP: When?
Colgan: Outside the Legion one night at the camper. Yeah, I told him the whole story. He told me about the shit he could get me in cause he was the Sheriff.
RCMP: Did you tell Gerry the facts as you told us, or was there certain things you kept from him?
Colgan: I think I pretty well told him everything.

No one in town could have seen a brighter shade of red. Sheriff Wilson was flushed, beads of sweat lightly dripping off his temples. His seat, directly below and in front of the judge, was in full view. All eyes were on the bespectacled elderly man and all he could do was sit there stone-faced, blushing, staring off into the distance. Defence and Crown counsel tried desperately to feign no reaction.

When Mr. Justice Schwartz later asked if the sheriff might be called as a witness, the defence and Crown said yes. The short, chubby sheriff, his eyes lowered, was excused from his duties and quickly darted out and removed his long, black robe. Later that day, the sheriff resumed his duties after the Crown and defence said they had no intention of calling him to testify. There would have been no purpose for the defence to call Wilson because they had already shown Colgan to be inconsistent, and possibly a liar. And the Crown obviously wouldn't have wanted to dispute their own evidence with Colgan by bringing the sheriff up to refute it.

Brodsky kept going after Colgan, asking him why he'd placed Manger in the back seat in his confession to Wilson. Colgan kept saying the sheriff had gotten his words wrong. Brodsky finally suggested that Colgan had said Manger was there because, like everyone else in town, he thought Norm Manger, not his brother Jim, had committed suicide.

> Brodsky: You see, Mr. Colgan, my suggestion to you clearly is that the reason you put Norman Manger in the back seat instead of you is because at that time you thought the stabbing took place in the car, and Manger couldn't deny it because he was dead, had committed suicide, and that's the reason you told the story.

Colgan denied it. He knew that Jim, not Norm, had

committed suicide. Later that day, a reporter covering the trial began chatting with the front desk clerk at a local hotel and said how shocked she was that the sheriff had known about the killing. But the clerk was unfazed, replying, "It's nothing we ain't heard before."

Brodsky then accused Colgan of writing out a statement to his lawyer just after he had gained his deal of immunity, claiming that Johnston had talked the girl into getting into the car, rather than forcing her. Colgan first agreed with this version, but then changed his story seconds later. No, he said; Johnston had forced her into the car after all. Brodsky suggested that Colgan had originally told his lawyer the truth. He changed his story when it became apparent his version didn't match what the cops had.

> Brodsky: What did you mean when you said to the police, "Dwayne got out and talked her into coming to a party. I looked up and down the street and as far as I know nobody saw us pick her up."
> Colgan: That Dwayne got out and tried to talk her into coming to a party and we didn't want to see anybody or any witnesses see her get into the car.
> Brodsky: Because she was forced into the car?
> Colgan: Yes.

After jousting with Brodsky, Colgan was worn out and in danger of blowing his assignment to nail Johnston as the killer. He'd already admitted to blaming Johnston to get off a murder charge and then told different versions of the killing to police, Veito, and Wilson.

Brodsky's toughest job was trying to dispute Andrea Wiwcharuk's testimony. Brodsky kept cross-examining Wiwcharuk but couldn't break her down – she knew what she'd heard and when she'd heard it. She fully admitted she hadn't known who Johnston was talking about; it was just something that had stuck in her mind at the age of fourteen. "When I heard the comments, I didn't know what he was talking about,'' Wiwcharuk snapped at Brodsky. ''I'm not going to go and rat to a police officer and say, 'Hey, guess what I heard.' ''

Brodsky seemed spooked; he couldn't break her down or show any substantial inconsistencies in her testimony. One argument Brodsky did present was that if Wiwcharuk had indeed heard the statement, why hadn't she been shocked? Why didn't other people at the party hear it? It seemed as if she had just pounded the last nail into Johnston's coffin. There was tension in the courtroom as some spectators speculated that Johnston must have been the killer. Otherwise, why would he brag about it?

Initially, Scurfield's cross-examination was much more friendly towards Colgan than Brodsky's. Perhaps Scurfield didn't want to get on the bad side of Colgan right away, since he was being so co-operative – and he wasn't pointing the finger at his client. (''I told Scurfield my client would co-operate but not to push him,'' Don MacIver said later.)

Scurfield asked Colgan if he was sure it was Johnston who'd forced the girl into the car. He referred to the preliminary hearing in July when Colgan had testified he'd been too drunk to remember exactly which person had forced her to get in. ''And your memory, as I understand it now, between July of 1987 and November of 1987, has improved. Is that what you're saying?'' Scurfield asked him. Colgan replied that it had.

Under this cross-examination, Colgan told the court that since 1970, he'd experimented with a lot of drugs including marijuana, LSD, blotter acid, and mescalin, and that he sold MDA, which street people called the love drug. The cross-examination at this point provided a rare moment of levity in the tense courtroom.

Scurfield: So during those years you were even a drug trafficker, is that right?
Colgan: I didn't get too far, I did most of it myself.
Scurfield: I didn't say you were a good drug trafficker,

but you were a drug trafficker, isn't that right?
Colgan: Yes.

Everyone in the courtroom, including the accused, laughed. After hours of gruelling cross-examination, Scurfield had managed to lighten up the tense air in the courtroom. But it was short-lived.

Scurfield continued his questioning and got Colgan to admit that the illegal drugs were hallucinogens, which really bent his mind around when he took them. He no longer took them but now took tranquillizers daily. He said he had taken some before coming to testify in court.

Trying to break down what was left of his credibility, Scurfield attacked Colgan's memory. He had waited sixteen years to write down what had happened that night.

Scurfield: But the fact is that you never wrote all this down in any detail until sixteen years after it happened. Isn't that fair to say?
Colgan: Yes.
Scurfield: And that's a lot of liquor and a lot of pills later, isn't it, Mr. Colgan?
Colgan: Yes.

Colgan, a man who made drinking and drugs his full-time occupational hazard, said when he got the DTs he wanted to die. He was about to confirm what Brodsky had touched on earlier about tailoring his story to match what the police knew – and wanted him to say. But Scurfield was much more direct when asking Colgan about getting his deal of immunity on March 10, 1987.

Scurfield: And that's why you were in the Crown Attorney's office from ten o'clock until four o'clock on the day of your preliminary hearing, giving them a statement. Because you gave them all the detail you could. Is that right?
Colgan: We went over my statement, yes.

Scurfield: Yes, and they asked you questions every which way to Sunday, I bet, to see if they could get every detail out of you that you had by then. Is that fair to say?

Colgan: They wanted to match my story with theirs.

Scurfield: Well, we'll get to that, because it didn't match with some of the stories they had, did it?

Colgan: No.

Scurfield: It didn't match with some of the stories you told other people over the years, did it?

Colgan: I don't know about that.

Scurfield: Well, they [RCMP] told you it didn't match. Let me put it that way.

Colgan: Yeah, okay.

Whether he realized it or not, Colgan had just admitted to trying to match his story to the police's, presumably to suit the physical evidence at the scene.

After already having laid the groundwork that Colgan was somewhat less than a pillar of society, Scurfield started to examine Colgan about the role his client, Houghton, had played in the killing. Colgan, who couldn't describe him enough times as "a nice guy," said he and Houghton hadn't set out to take Betty Osborne by force that night and the pair were disgusted by this whole violent mess Johnston had gotten them involved in. Colgan testified that Houghton had told Johnston not to hurt the girl.

Scurfield: And there's thumping and there's banging out there when you three are talking and Jim is saying, "We've got to do something." Right?

Colgan: Yes.

Colgan said he had no reason to believe that nice, neighbourly Jim Houghton had turned into a maniac with a screwdriver. Jim was just a nice, big old guy who happened to be cruising around one night with a couple of friends and ended up in the company of a frenzied killer. It was a simple case of being in the wrong place at the wrong time, Colgan explained.

Colgan insisted during this cross-examination that Houghton had gotten out of the car and then Johnston had come back for a screwdriver. Since Scurfield couldn't get Colgan to admit that Houghton had gotten out of the car after Johnston had pulled out the screwdriver, he painted Colgan as being somewhat confused and disoriented about the time because he'd been drinking so heavily.

> Scurfield: When you got back on the road, it was you who told the people in the back, or Dwayne or whoever it was, to throw out the screwdriver, wasn't it?
> Colgan: I'm not sure. I think it could have been me.

Colgan had his story well rehearsed. He had spent several days in the Wescana Hotel in The Pas as police and the Crown rammed the testimony into his head. Each time they cross-examined him in different ways. The Crown was trying to make sure of two things: that Colgan would be sober for the trial and that he had his story down pat.

In a particularly clever move, Scurfield read out almost the entire statement Colgan had made to the sheriff, to show that the man Colgan was really afraid of was Johnston – whom he feared would do him bodily harm – if he told police about the killing. It seemed strange that Colgan would fear Johnston, who was out of province at the time, but the tactic worked perfectly for Scurfield. The prosecution, blow by blow, was losing its case against Houghton. Scurfield, quite masterfully, was gaining ground with the jury.

Wilson's statement was taken by Urbanoski on April 2, 1986, eight or nine years after he had heard Colgan's version of the events.

It would be the summer of either 1977 or 1978 and I had occasion to speak with a fellow by the name of Lee Colgan. I've known Lee for quite some time since about 1951. There is an age difference between us and we never chummed together but I knew him through his parents and the Legion. Lee was in the Legion on this occasion and when I arrived I sat at his table. There may have been someone else there to start with but when closing time rolled around we were alone. As best as I can recall, someone had ordered a drink for Lee, a screwdriver, and this apparently seemed to bother him. At closing time I invited Lee to my camper truck, which was parked on the street. We had a few drinks in the camper and Lee started to talk about the murder. He didn't seem depressed and wasn't crying about the incident but seemed bothered by the fact the screwdriver drink had arrived at his table. When Lee started talking about the murder, I asked him why or how he got involved in this. He told me they were just driving around after the Legion closed. He didn't say what time and from what I can remember he said someone in the car knew Osborne and she got into the car willingly and this would have taken place somewhere nearby the Legion but the exact location wasn't told to me. I believe he told me it was on 4th Street between the Legion and the railway station. Lee told me upon my questioning that she was killed because, ''she didn't want to screw for us.'' He stated that the body was dumped in the bush at the pumphouse. He made no mention of whether or not she was alive when they arrived at the pumphouse nor did he say anything about her clothing being on or off during the killing. He told me he was driving his father's car – the white Chrysler – on the night that this happened and that night he had been drinking. He never said anything about being drunk and never indicated if liquor was being consumed in the vehicle. Lee stated that Johnston and Manger were in the back and Johnston was the one who did the actual stabbing. Colgan told me that he was afraid of Johnston and this is why he didn't stop the killing. He claims he is afraid to go to the police to tell them the story of this murder as he feels Johnston will do him bodily harm. He made no mention whether any additional stabbing took place outside the vehicle or if she had been beaten prior to the stabbing. I asked to what Houghton's involvement in this and he told me that he [Houghton] stayed in the car while the body was being removed to the pumphouse and was apparently the only other one in the front seat with Colgan. When Lee and I were talking about who was in the vehicle with him, I believe him to be talking about Dwayne Johnston and Jim Houghton and the Manger boy – I didn't know his first name – and that's when he told me he was afraid of Johnston. I told Colgan he should tell the police about this murder instead of me because I couldn't help him in this matter. That's when he told me that he was afraid of Johnston. At this point in the conversation I asked him where everybody was now. He told me Houghton was in Alberta employed as a salesman, Johnston was up at Lakehead and I think he said Manger had committed suicide. Lee was upset by the fact that he believed an RCMP officer was the one that was buying the screwdriver drinks and felt it would drive him crazy.

Just when spectators in the courtroom thought they had had enough of the sheriff, more scandal about Wilson came out. Scurfield relentlessly examined Colgan, asking him to speculate why the sheriff had one version of the killing and Colgan another. "I don't know," Colgan replied. "Maybe he was just as drunk as I was when I was telling him."

Then Scurfield turned his attention to whether Colgan had seen Houghton do anything at all that night to hurt Betty Osborne.

Scurfield: When it comes right down to it, even based on what you believe happened, even if that's true, even if your memory is correct, and I'm not saying you're a liar, but even if you're correct after all these years and all the problems you've had, you never did see Jim Houghton touch this girl, did you?
Colgan: No.

Colgan admitted it was he who'd touched the girl's breasts, held her down while Johnston swung at her, and stuffed her back into the car at the Houghton cabin.

Scurfield: All that Jim did was tell Dwayne on the way to the pumphouse to stop and then get out of the car and try and stop him, but it was too late. Isn't that right?
Colgan: Yes.

On that very positive note, Scurfield ended his case.

After all the evidence had been cross-examined and re-examined by the Crown, it was time for the defence to decide whether to call Johnston or Houghton to testify on his own behalf.

No doubt Brodsky and Scurfield had kept that option until the end to see how things progressed during the trial. No lawyer would want to expose a client to gruelling cross-examination by the Crown unless they absolutely had to, especially the type conducted by Dangerfield. And a question neither of the accused could answer with any credibility was why they had remained silent for sixteen years if they were innocent.

While the two defence attorneys talked with their clients in the consulting room, Johnston recalled remarking: "Why don't we get our shit together and say what really happened. It's gone too far." According to Johnston, Scurfield replied: "Look, this town's on trial and someone's going to pay. If you take the stand I'll put Jim up there and he'll confirm Colgan's story."

Houghton, who hadn't exchanged so much as a hello to Johnston throughout the trial, remained silent when Scurfield announced his intentions. That, Johnston said, is when Brodsky convinced him he would be guaranteed a conviction if he took the stand. At least by keeping his mouth shut, he had a chance. Or so he thought.

CHAPTER FOURTEEN

Before Justice Sidney Schwartz charged the jury on December 1, 1987, they heard day-long closing arguments from the prosecution and the defence. This would be the Crown's last chance to plea for two convictions. It was Brodsky and Scurfield's last line of defence, their final hope for an acquittal.

Crown Attorney George Dangerfield had told the jury at the outset that the crime had been murder in the Crown's view if "one or both of them killed Helen Betty Osborne in the course of attempting to rape her or some other sexual assault or killed Helen Betty Osborne in an effort to escape responsibility for having done what they did in the course of assaulting her."

Dangerfield tried to convince jurors that Colgan's testimony was believable not only because he had been there but also because he was willing to admit that he had sexually assaulted Osborne, pinned her arms down, and did nothing to stop the killing. The Crown's logic was that since Colgan wasn't willing to lie on the stand to make himself look good, he wouldn't lie to protect any one else. "And he didn't do anything, did he, to stop Johnston's attack, and he was sitting within touching distance of Johnston and could have a better opportunity than perhaps Houghton . . . And Colgan may have been reluctant to admit some of these things, but admit them he did," Dangerfield said.

He told the all-white jury to look at other facts supporting Colgan's testimony, such as physical evidence found at the scene, blood, fabric and hair uncovered in the car, and the fourth man's testimony, that of Manger. The prosecutor must have known his case against Johnston had gone well during the trial and the jury wouldn't have a difficult time convicting him of murder.

However, the Crown's case against Houghton was thin. Houghton's defence had probably raised some grave doubts about his guilt in the jurors' minds: Dangerfield's arguments had to be convincing. He had to give the jury something, anything, to erase that reasonable doubt.

As he stood gripping his pen on both ends, Dangerfield told the jurors that just because Houghton might have told Johnston to stop hurting Betty Osborne that didn't mean he hadn't helped kill her when he got out of the car.

If Houghton is, if I may use a vulgarism, a good guy, what on earth was he doing driving to the pump-house? . . . Had they gone back to The Pas, you may think, had they gone back and got her some coffee, straightened her up, apologized to her, taken her home, do you think that anyone would have taken any real serious note of her complaint at that stage? . . But apparently this man, Houghton, who was so anxious that nothing should happen, he did exactly the opposite. He took the girl to an even lonelier place than his cabin where there was no one around with a man he could see and hear was physically attacking this girl, causing her to scream and cry out against him, ripping her clothes.

Now, members of the jury, if Houghton was out there to stop what ultimately became a murder, what on earth did he do? She was alive when Houghton left the car and Helen Betty Osborne was dead when he came back. What did he do? He's a big man. You can see looking at him he's bigger than Johnston. Would

it have been such a trick to stop a man who had
mad and was beating up a girl?

After finishing with Houghton, Dangerfield confidently
moved on to Johnston. He told the jury that some of the
most damning evidence against Johnston had been provided by Andrea Wiwcharuk's's testimony regarding the
party she'd attended when she'd overheard Johnston
boasting. "So what do you think Johnston was talking
about. Screwdriver? Stabbed her and stabbed her? Tore
the car apart? What could he have been talking about
except the murder of Helen Betty Osborne?'' Dangerfield
asked. Looking self-assured, Dangerfield asked the jury
for verdicts of guilty against Houghton and Johnston.

Brodsky was next to make his closing arguments, most
of which consisted of telling the jury that Colgan's testimony wasn't credible. "The fact of the matter is that
the way they broke open this case was to charge one guy
with murder. And that's squeezing him pretty hard. And
they said, 'Okay my boy, there's blood on your car,
there's a brassière in your car, torn parts of clothes in
your car, your car was out there and you're charged with
murder. Now you've got a way to get out of this. We
want Johnston.' ''

Leaning over the wooden podium, Brodsky, looking
more like a university professor, reminded jurors how
Colgan hadn't blamed Johnston for the killing right after
it had happened, but that he'd taken his time. Brodsky
reread testimony from the trial in which he'd asked Colgan when he had remembered Johnston was the killer.
"Well, I didn't blame Archie Johnston, Dwayne Archie
Johnston at the beginning,'' Colgan said. "It was later
on that you got around to blaming Dwayne, wasn't it?''
Brodsky had asked. "It was later on when I remembered
a few things,'' Colgan replied.

Describing him as a slippery fellow, Brodsky tried
relentlessly, mentioning one point after another, to convince the jury that Colgan's evidence couldn't be be-

lieved. Brodsky's argument that Colgan's testimony wasn't credible or that he was a liar seemed quite plausible, and one the jury might readily accept. Even the accusation that Colgan sold his soul to put Johnston in jail was believable. But the one question the jury would have to deal with was this: If Johnston wasn't the killer, then who was? If Brodsky had his own theory, he never shared it with the jury.

While it appeared Brodsky gained some ground by disputing Colgan's testimony, he didn't successfully dispute Wiwcharuk's testimony, the most damning evidence against Johnston. Ironically, he pointed to Colgan to dispute her memory of the facts. Brodsky also mentioned Manger, who didn't remember the comment, and still others who were in a position to hear Johnston's boast but didn't testify in court, such as Rick Colgan, Arlee White, and Bob Halliday. He pointed out how odd it was that no one else remembered hearing Johnston's comment at the party except for Wiwcharuk. "I mean, does that sound logical, reasonable, comprehensible? There's no reaction. There's no stunned silence. There's no teasing, 'Oh, come on.' There's no questions, there's no anything. You couldn't control such a story," Brodsky told the jury.

Then he presented the jury with several possible variations of the killing. First, he tried to convince jurors that the killer might not necessarily have known what he was doing when he stabbed Betty Osborne fifty times, cracking her skull. "If you wanted to kill somebody, would you kill him fifty times, would you kick him like that, unless you don't know what you're doing, that you're in such a frenzy that you don't know what's happening," Brodsky asked.

His second theory was that the man, whichever one it was, came back for a screwdriver because Osborne, during the course of a sexual assault, had temporarily fled towards the bush. "That girl ran away, and the reason she was way down over there was because she ran away, and the reason for the screwdriver was to go and get her back and say, 'Hey, you can't run around like that, lady, with no clothes on cause there's going to be trouble. Get back in the car and settle down.' "

Another theory was that the killing had taken place with the four men in the car. Brodsky told jurors to look at the evidence of clothing – some of it was strewn along the highway, the rest of it hidden under rocks at the shore close to where the body was found. "The problem that we have is that one person tells us a story because he can't do the time, and the police tell him he has to blame Dwayne Johnston, so he does, for which he gets off a murder charge. You have to now decide whether or not you want to transfer what the police were going to put on Colgan onto my client."

Some of Brodsky's arguments were convincing enough to prompt jurors occasionally to nod their heads in agreement. When the attention of one female juror wandered to this fit, handsome man, he would flash a gentle smile in her direction.

But even though Brodsky tended to play what some lawyers call jury games, John Scurfield's were more obvious. Scurfield usually delivered his closing arguments with the smoothness of a natural-born salesman. And jurors loved it.

Earlier that day, the judge had denied Scurfield's motion for a directed verdict of not guilty for his client, saying there was sufficient evidence to let the jury decide.

Scurfield began his closing arguments by asking the jury, who were tired after listening for several hours, to pay close attention to him because Houghton was on trial for his life. Young, sharp, and articulate, Scurfield appeared humble to the jury several times; he portrayed himself as an upstanding person who just wanted what was in the interests of justice. "I'm not a perfect human being or a perfect lawyer," he told the jury. "And when I present a case, or when I present an argument I might miss something. In fact I know I missed something. There's twelve of you and there's obviously a piece of evidence or there may even be an argument that I don't advance.''

Good intentions aside, Scurfield told the jurors to look at all the evidence, no matter how unbelievable some of it may have been. ''You can't say, well, I don't believe Colgan, something else might have happened. You have to go with what you've got as evidence,'' he said. ''If you rely on the evidence that Mr. Colgan gave, that evidence doesn't lead to a conclusion that Mr. Houghton did this crime. It leads to a decision that he's probably not guilty. And I think it makes your job with respect to Houghton as opposed to Johnston a lot easier.''

Using various examples, Scurfield explained how all of the evidence against Houghton was circumstantial. He pointed to the footprints, which weren't conclusive, the murder weapon without fingerprints, and the testimony of one man, Colgan. ''The first thing to remember is that there are two reasons why you may find that his [Colgan's] evidence is unreliable. The first is and the most obvious one is that maybe he's not telling you the truth.''

The second reason, Scurfield said, was that Colgan might believe that what he'd told the jury was true, but since he'd been so drunk, he probably didn't have the details straight.

Scurfield, looking earnest, said that even if the jury were to believe Colgan, they would undoubtedly come to the conclusion that Houghton was innocent. ''The Crown has proved that he's [Houghton] not guilty through their only witness, Lee Colgan. And that doesn't upset Mr. Dangerfield. We're not here for his personal concerns. If the witness he's got in essence exonerates Mr. Houghton of the crime, then so be it.''

Scurfield told the jurors that the Crown had no evidence to show that Houghton acted in concert with Johnston to kill Betty Osborne. ''Well, what evidence is there of that? One would expect that if the Crown hadn't given immunity to Mr. Colgan, and had charged him, that you might be concerned that Colgan maybe did act in concert with Johnston.'' He said Houghton was the only one of the three men who had the courage to try to stop Johnston from hurting Betty Osborne.

He told jurors to not speculate on what happened when he'd gotten out of the car because, for all they knew, he could have been relieving himself. Scurfield kept on pushing the blame onto Johnston, as if there was no doubt he was the killer. ''I say to you that this must have been a frenzied killing, a drunken maniac. It's the only way to explain the number of wounds. What are the odds? Think about that for a minute, of two human beings flipping out entirely at the same time? . . . And who's likely to flip out?''

But Scurfield even went a little farther, perhaps too far, when he explained in detail how Dwayne Johnston could have killed Betty Osborne. He said that Johnston was fighting with the girl and when he went to fetch the screwdriver from the car, she saw that he was going for a weapon, and ran for her life over to the mounds.

He follows her with the screwdriver, running after her. He catches her before the mound, just after the mound, it doesn't matter, and they start to fight. Only now he's fighting with a screwdriver in his hand. He's punching at her with a screwdriver in his hand, hitting her in the chest area. Scurfield explained how Johnston kept stabbing at Osborne before she, beaten and bleeding, fell to the ground, creating the first set of blood stains.

And when she falls to the ground – because he's in a frenzy – because he's completely lost control because of the drink and the anger that's confusing him, he kicks at her, kicks her in the head and causes those terrible fractures that you've heard about.

And either because she's fallen on her face or his kicks roll her over or whatever, she's on her back, and then he falls to his knees and he stabs and he stabs, and finally with one blow, one very, very hard blow, causes the blow which enters the brain. And he gets up and he stands there and he's in shock about what he's done. And he thinks, as far as a complete drunk can think, and he drags her, picks her up by the hands, drags her back into the bush and drops her.

And by the time Houghton had gotten out of the car, Scurfield said, Johnston was in a frenzy, stabbing Osborne repeatedly in the darkness of the bush. Houghton stood outside the car in a drunken daze. Then, he said, Colgan yelled for the two men and Johnston replied, "Just a minute" and ran out from the bushes. When Houghton asked him what was going on, he told him that she was dead. "He [Johnston] grabs the clothes and runs off and Houghton's standing there. He didn't kill her. He didn't help him kill her."

Calling that a better theory than the Crown's, Scurfield told the jury that common sense dictated that Houghton hadn't killed Betty Osborne. "Jim Houghton may have to live with the shame of being there, and I'm not saying he's morally blameworthy, that he should be complimented for his behaviour on that night, and I don't think he compliments himself. But he's guilty, with respect, of misjudgment and perhaps immaturity for getting involved with the wrong people on the wrong night but he's not guilty of murder . . . On behalf of Jim Houghton and on behalf of his family, I urge you to find him not guilty."

By this time it was almost 3:30 P.M., and the jury, which had just returned from a break, began listening to Judge Schwartz's charge. During the four-hour charge, jurors listened attentively, occasionally nodding their heads in agreement.

At the outset, he told the jury in a forceful, decisive manner to have no sympathy for Johnston and Houghton just because they were married men with children or because the murder had been committed sixteen years ago. "Having children and being married is no defence to a crime," Schwartz told them.

Schwartz went over almost all the twenty-three witnesses' testimony during the seven-day trial, explaining in detail the difference between expert and ordinary witnesses and what testimony was less credible than others. Throughout his charge, he stressed over and over again how dangerous Colgan's testimony was because he was an alcoholic and had so much to gain – his freedom. Schwartz pointed to Colgan's three versions of the killing – one he had told to the sheriff, another to the police over the years, and a third in the witness box.

Even though Colgan had been there during the killing, Schwartz said, it was risky to rely on his evidence. "It may be that Colgan was lying when he gave that evidence, or that he was mistaken in saying that the person fighting with the deceased was the accused, Johnston." Johnston nodded his head approvingly in the prisoner's dock.

He also warned the jurors that Manger's testimony was equally unsafe. "Manger testified that he concocted a false alibi, that he actually told people at the time the case was being investigated that he was elsewhere. . . . He's an admitted liar in order to escape the consequences of his being there."

He described evidence of footprints as "uncomfortable" because the evidence of Harold Bielert, the indentification officer at the time, had been strongly disputed. There was some confusion in court as to whether there had been two sets of footprints leading up to the body.

Schwartz explained that Bielert, an expert witness, first said he had nothing in his sixteen-year-old notes about footprints on either side of the drag marks from Osborne's heels. But upon further questioning, he'd said he remembered footprints being on both sides of Betty Osborne's body. He was asked whether he had remembered that after talking to Constable Knight and he said no.

While Knight, chief investigator at the time, said there had been two distinct sets of prints, it had been Bielert's responsibility to preserve them, at least on paper. Two sets of prints obviously would have meant that two people had dragged Betty Osborne to die in the bush. Needless to say, Bielert's forgetfulness might have raised a reasonable doubt in the minds of the jury as to whether two people had dragged Osborne to her death. It would be a big help to the jury when deciding Houghton's involvement.

The Queen's Bench judge was very careful to separate Johnston's involvement from Houghton's and stressed that evidence against one wasn't evidence against the other. "I've said twice, three times, four times, it bears a final repeating: it is most important that you treat each accused separately."

But the judge's charge seemed to get complicated and somewhat cumbersome when he told the jury they could find either Johnston or Houghton guilty of murder, guilty of manslaughter, or not guilty. While he obviously wanted just to simplify the intricacies of the law for the jury, he ended up making things even more complex. They could not find the men guilty of the Crown's charge of first-degree murder, he explained, because they were bound by the laws of 1971 when the crime was committed. At the time, there had been only capital murder for the killing of police officers, prison officials, and the like and non-capital murder for the killing of ordinary citizens.

Completing his charge, the judge gave the jurors one final warning before they broke for dinner at 6:15 P.M. "Consider the evidence fully and fairly without prejudice and without sympathy."

Moments later, counsel from both sides said that, while the charge had been fair, they had several points they wanted to discuss. Among a number of things, Scurfield told Schwartz he had been too forceful when stressing how the jurors should dismiss his theory that the killing had occurred without Houghton's involvement.

"I was attempting to protect the interests of the ac-

cused, Johnston,'' Schwartz replied. "Perhaps your sub-
tlety was lost on the jury as it was lost on me. And it
seemed to me that what you were doing was putting on
to the shoulder of Johnston the whole of the responsibility.'' (Schwartz later described Scurfield's closing address as "horribly unfair'' to Johnston.)

The judge briefly recharged the jury on a few minor
points before he stressed once again that they should be
very cautious of Colgan's testimony. "I said to be careful
to make sure that you believe him, if you do, because
he may have had a tailored story; he may have just created
the story to meet the physical evidence that was there.''

By law the judge had to instruct the jury not to give
too much credence to Colgan's testimony because he had
so much to gain by giving it. But it appeared as if Schwartz,
too, had tremendous difficulty believing Colgan's drunken recollections. It occasionally seemed as if the judge
was thinking out loud, confirming for himself as much
as the jury how unreliable Colgan's testimony was.

Somehow, Schwartz managed to impress even Johnston, the man who was convicted. "I like Judge Schwartz,''
Johnston said in prison afterwards. "He seemed like a
very fair guy. He does a good job.''

The jury broke for dinner at 7:30 that night before
beginning their deliberations but when they came back
at 9:00 P.M., they were too tired to deliberate and wanted
to adjourn for the night. The next morning they resumed
shortly after 9:30 A.M.

The courtroom was packed. Spectators shuffled in the
hallways. Some had nodded off; others made phone calls.
The fifty-odd individuals waiting for the verdict expected
it to be a long haul.

No one – Crown prosecutors, judges, or defence lawyers – can ever predict what a jury will decide or how
long it will take to do so. But the evidence seemed so
strong against Johnston that many spectators suspected
his fate had been decided over the previous day's dinner.
They suspected that Houghton's fate would be tough to

decide since the Crown's case on him was thin and circumstantial at best. And then there was Colgan's
endorsement of him as ''such a nice guy.'' Everything
seemed to have gone so well for him.

But to everyone's amazement the jury, looking relaxed
and well rested, returned shortly after 10:00 A.M. that
morning, ready to give the verdict.

''Members of the jury, have you reached your verdict?
If so, who shall speak for you?'' the court clerk asked.

The male foreman stood up and said: ''I will.''

''How say you? Do you find the prisoner, Dwayne
Archie Johnston, guilty or not guilty?''

''Guilty,'' said the jury foreman.

Johnston frowned, gazed at the courtroom ceiling, looked
at his wife and then down at his feet, shaking his head
in disbelief. His friend, fellow biker, Wilf Cudmore,
began openly weeping in the courtroom. A gasp from
Johnston's wife, Patricia, broke the courtroom silence
when her husband's sentence of life imprisonment with
no eligibility of parole for ten years was pronounced.

His co-accused smiled widely at the jury after he was
found not guilty in the killing of Betty Osborne and then
sat anxiously in the prisoner's dock until it was time to
go. It was difficult to tell who was happier with the verdict
– Houghton, his sister Donna, or his lawyer, John Scurfield, who seemed ready to celebrate in the courtroom
halls.

As Houghton was discharged from the prisoner's dock,
Schwartz told Johnston that the years since the murder
must have been very unpleasant for him. ''Spending sixteen years having that on your mind, having it on your
conscience for sixteen years, can't have been a very pleasant
sixteen years of life, but they were years of life which
Miss Osborne was deprived of.''

He explained he hadn't made an order to lengthen the
time Johnston had to serve before becoming eligible for
parole because Johnston had been burdened with a guilty
conscience. ''Sixteen years of a secret or not-so-secret

murder on your conscience combined with life imprisonment with no eligibility for parole for the next ten years makes it at least twenty-six years, during which time you've either walked around with a crime on your conscience privately or during which you won't walk around except in custody, with the public knowing what you did.''

CHAPTER FIFTEEN

With the verdict came a wealth of emotions, ranging from happiness to disgust and outrage.

The most extreme reaction was that of the victim's mother, Justine Osborne. She squeezed her fists, hammered them on her knees, and then shook her head in disgust as the not-guilty verdict was read out to Houghton. To her, Houghton was smiling for all the wrong reasons: he was free after allegedly helping to kill her daughter and then dragging the body into the bush, leaving her like a piece of garbage.

She was angry, fed up and felt betrayed by the white man's justice system again. "It was hard for me," Justine Osborne said later. "I don't know how come the other three got free of it and only one went to jail. For me, I think it's not right. I didn't really know what to think of the people at The Pas and I didn't really know anybody from there but I think that the people at The Pas didn't care anything about the murder of my daughter."

Justine Osborne had every right to feel that way. To her, this was the most extreme example one could imagine of justice not being done. All the elements were there: the fat lawyer who'd instructed the four to keep quiet, the hard-drinking sheriff who'd known all along what had happened yet had done nothing and the town that had kept quiet and shielded the killers for so long.

It was as if Betty Osborne was incidental, something

unpleasant that was dealt with only because it made the police and public feel uneasy. As far as Natives could tell, the case had been "solved" simply because it began to make people feel uncomfortable – it looked like the white people's conscience had caught up with them. There would be many tears shed for Betty Osborne – some by her eleven brothers and sisters, but by many Natives across Canada.

To them, the Osborne case was the other side of the coin: four white men got away with a crime for years because the victim was Native and her death apparently wasn't important enough to investigate thoroughly. The stereotype of the corrupt, conceited, superior white man was confirmed yet again. This time he was telling Natives they shouldn't complain. Instead of moaning about the one conviction, Natives should be happy the case even got to court. It was a case of like it or leave it.

But band chiefs and Native leaders throughout Manitoba chose neither. They joined forces, demanding a full public inquiry. Countless stories and editorials would appear in Winnipeg's two daily newspapers, Canada's national news magazine *Maclean's*, on CBC's *fifth estate* program, in *The Globe and Mail*, and in just about every newspaper across Canada. And the theme running through them all was similar to the opinion of Norway House Band Chief Allan Ross, who said: "They're covering up. There's a lot of undesirable elements to this problem. There a heavy element of racism in this and it would not have happened, in my opinion, to a white person or anybody else other than an Indian person. It's disgusting."

The trial and Houghton's eventual release also triggered anger in The Pas Indian Band Chief Oscar Lathlin. "I'm disgusted that three out of four got away and one of the men bought his own freedom," he said. "Even from Day 1 we [band councillors] were predicting the outcome." Band leaders everywhere reacted similarly, adding to the strained relations in the province. The tension is still felt today.

Although some whites sided with the Natives, many people, especially in The Pas, considered newspaper and television reports biased and sensational. They said the townspeople were actually wonderful, kind people who'd been upset in 1971 about Osborne's murder but had felt too helpless to do anything. She had been killed at a time when criminals constantly seemed to be getting off and this was just another example, they said.

The townspeople did qualify that belief, of course, by saying that perhaps some people had known and could have done something about it, but it was still all probably hearsay evidence. That apathetic view, apparently, was their explanation for not going to police after hearing the murder confessions but it was an unconvincing argument from a white or Native standpoint.

Lee Colgan was interviewed on a half-hour CBC television documentary that followed up on the case, broadcast in Winnipeg. He granted the interview in part because he felt he was victimized by the newspapers and he wanted to tell his story. The interview was also used a few months later on a *fifth estate* program.

Colgan said he didn't want to talk to the newspapers because they didn't write articles he liked and because they weren't "nice" to him. His father slammed the front door of his home in one reporter's face. He, like many people in The Pas, blamed all of his son's ills and the town's racial problems on the newspapers. Apparently, the press was supposed to feel sorry for Lee Colgan and reward him for finally telling what he calls the true story of the murder as he had done on TV:

> It was just going out for a drunken car ride when you're young, which we did several times and everybody else did. And it turned into a horror story, I guess. Nobody actually knew what was happening . . . I don't know what happened outside the car because I wasn't outside. But I knew shortly after and since then, I don't know how to explain it; it's been hell . . . We were

scared, very scared. I didn't know how to react to it so I just did what everybody else seemed to do. I just went along . . . They [police and the Crown] did everything that I was hoping they would. Johnston is the killer.

Colgan's comments about the murder during the TV interview were as unconvincing as they had been in the courtroom. And many townspeople in The Pas were shaking their heads in amazement – the story Colgan told in court didn't remotely resemble any of the dozen or so versions he'd been telling them over drinks for the past sixteen years. Some of them suspected all those years that Colgan had done the deed, just as they had suspected Johnston.

Perhaps no one was more in the dark regarding this murder than Johnston's wife, Patricia, who steadfastly believed in his innocence throughout the trial. Once the verdict was announced, she demanded to know why he hadn't taken the witness stand to tell his side of the story. "I said, 'Why didn't you get up there and say your piece?'" Patricia recalled. "But the lawyer told him it was the wrong time and to not get up there and incriminate himself. I think he should have gotten up there regardless and said something or did something. I think he regrets it now because telling the truth could have helped."

But she stuck by his side anyway. Patricia did not believe her husband killed Osborne. "I think they pinned it on him," she said afterwards. "He's there because they wanted Dwayne Johnston. I just wish the others would have told the truth and then this whole mess could have been avoided and they could have got the right guys."

Patricia told one of Johnston's biker friends about how depressed she was about having to wait until 1996 for her husband's release. The friend told her that he, as well as the rest of the biker gang, would be willing to take turns satisfying her sexual needs in the interim. He sympathized with her, he said, and explained that Johnston's prison sentence was an unreasonably long time to wait. Taken aback and disgusted, Patricia politely declined.

Houghton, meanwhile, drove home with a handful of newspaper reports of the trial, just in case his wife was interested. But Shannon said she hadn't read the newspapers and had never discussed the trial with him after he returned home. Everything returned to normal. "I'm not a worrier," Shannon said later. "And I didn't want to talk about it – I know my husband's innocent."

Manger might have expected to feel relief that a terrible burden had been lifted once the trial was over. But according to girlfriend Linda Hardy, the murder continues to haunt him. "He gets upset and shakes and everything whenever it's brought up," she said. "Sometimes I worry that he's going to commit suicide, just like his brother did."

EPILOGUE

Had the four men taken lawyer D'Arcy Bancroft's advice to keep a pact of silence, most likely they would have gotten away with murder. But Colgan was finally forced to relieve his conscience on a witness stand.

Houghton's another story. He supposedly bragged to one person of his involvement in the killing while vacationing with a friend in Las Vegas and the rumour, complete with graphic descriptions, made its way back to The Pas. But the man whom Houghton apparently told denied to RCMP that the conversation had ever taken place. Word had it that Houghton, in a drunken stupor, had also once boasted to a man in a bar in The Pas what he'd done during the killing.

Manger remained in a constant state of drunkenness after the killing, living as a vagrant. Like Colgan, he had a difficult time dealing with the murder of a Native woman on his conscience. He simply couldn't live with it.

And then there's Johnston, the man who today is serving a sentence of life imprisonment with no eligibility of parole for ten years. He sticks to his cell, staying away from Native inmates.

Since the trial, Colgan has remarried, sought counselling for his alcoholism and filed a grievance after being fired by CN Rail. Houghton has moved to Vancouver and is trying to start a new life. Manger, who recently got his driver's licence and has cut down on his drinking, plans to marry his common-law wife Linda Hardy one day. They're all men showing signs that they're trying to get on with their lives and forget that horrible night.

But only one of four men involved in the killing of Betty Osborne is doing time. Johnston takes upholstery classes at the maximum-security penitentiary in the hope of opening a shop when he gets out of prison. He hopes that day may come sooner than October 1996 – when he's eligible for parole. And so do his wife, Patricia, and his two children, Desiree and Jeremia.

Despite some of Patricia's bitter feelings towards her husband, she, for the most part is still sticking by him. Like many of his friends, she doesn't know the entire story about the night of the killing but believes Dwayne when he tells her it wasn't he who killed Betty Osborne and that Colgan was lying on the witness stand. (Patricia remains puzzled, saying her husband has given her three differing versions of the killing. In one, Johnston was trying to comfort Osborne as one of the others attacked her.) She believes two other men are responsible – one who held Osborne down and another who stabbed the Indian girl in a frenzy.

Johnston has never spoken on the record about the night of the killing, saying he doesn't want to jeopardize his parole. In an interview I conducted at the penitentiary, Johnston did give some details about what happened that night and revealed his views of the justice system regarding this particular case. Johnston said he remembers that Betty Osborne, whom he didn't know, got into the car where she was beaten in the front seat, while he and Manger sat in the back. Police, however, found no physical evidence that Osborne had been in the front seat, but plenty of evidence she'd been in the back.

Johnston is imprisoned at a maximum-security penitentiary which inmates commonly say is reserved for the "bad boys." He doesn't mix with others in the yard or in sports, staying secluded in his cell. Since CBC's *fifth estate* aired a documentary about the murder in March 1988, he has tried to stay out of trouble. Johnston said that just about every inmate in his block watched the program on their small black and white TVs and he could hear some of the Natives shouting angrily. He wishes, not surprisingly, that those inmates wouldn't believe everything they read in the newspapers or saw on TV – in essence all the evidence in court.

From the very beginning, Johnston didn't like the way the proceedings went. He said the prosecution's case presented in court didn't even remotely resemble what had happened during the killing and that it was tailor-made to implicate him. "I'm here because they wanted Dwayne Johnston," he said. But, then, he didn't testify on his own behalf.

As well, Johnston was angry at being denied bail, saying he would have helped construct a better defence. "I could have helped on my own investigation and got my own witnesses together instead of rotting at the re-mand centre," he explained. "They didn't even consider my situation when I wanted to get out on bail."

It was the senior Crown Attorney, George Dangerfield, who opposed bail. Johnston, naturally, isn't exactly en-amoured with the man that put him behind bars, describ-ing Dangerfield as a glory-seeker, as obnoxious and smug. "He painted me out to be some big biker-gang-type guy and I'm not," Johnston said. Since his appeal was dis-missed Johnston has been seeing himself as a victim, blaming others for his problems.

Johnston doesn't believe he had a fair trial either. His criticisms arise from the very beginning with the jury selection. He pointed out that one of the men on the panel used to be a bartender in The Pas. "He worked that bar and heard fifty stories about the murder a day," Johnston said. "How objective can he be?" As well, there was a woman on the jury from The Pas who had known and disliked him for years, he said.

The one person at his trial whom he did like was Justice Sidney Schwartz. He found him fair and balanced, and thought he seemed to see through Colgan's story.

Other than that, Johnston doesn't have a lot of good things to say. He has no idea where Andrea Wiwcharuk's testimony came from. He denies ever making any of the damning comments attributed to him. He doesn't even remember being at a party with her. Nor, he adds, does Bob Halliday, her supposed date who, Johnston said, didn't even own a trailer at the time the party is supposed to have taken place in it. Johnston is puzzled by the comment. He swears he followed Bancroft's advice and never said anything to anyone. Now it seems he's beginning to wish he had.

Johnston initially wanted to take the stand in his own defence but his lawyer advised him not to, a move Johnston regrets in hindsight. Deciding if and when to put the accused on the stand is one of the great arts of defence lawyers. A skilful cross-examination could reduce a perfectly innocent man to a glob of apparent guilt. But none of the four was perfectly innocent. In Johnston's case, we're talking about a man who said nothing to police about the killing for sixteen years and carried on merrily as if it never happened.

Suppose Johnston had taken the stand and pointed the finger at two other people. Had Houghton gone up next and confirmed Colgan's story – which pointed the finger at Johnston – to save his own skin, would the jury have been confused enough to acquit them both? We'll never know. But we do know that this was the type of jury that wouldn't have wanted to see the girl's death go unavenged. After sixteen years, someone had to pay.

Perhaps character witnesses to back up Johnston could have helped. Could the defence have built up a case strong enough to cast a stronger suspicion on Colgan's involvement and a reasonable doubt on that of Johnston?

Colgan, the man given immunity, made numerous slip-ups during the trial. The most telling was his admission that he had pointed the finger at Johnston just to get off of a murder charge. His testimony that Johnston was the killer wasn't very convincing. Even Justice Schwartz couldn't stress enough times in his charge to the jury that Colgan's evidence should be considered dangerous because he may have been lying just to match the physical evidence.

Once Colgan signed the deal of immunity on March 10, 1987, he had to maintain the story he'd peddled to gain his freedom. Otherwise the Crown could have turned around and charged him with perjury.

Colgan, a pathetically weak character, did more to raise suspicion about himself than he did to place guilt on Johnston. If Colgan was so innocent, why didn't he tell police what had happened at any time during all those years that the police had visited him? After the killing, he became a chronic alcoholic and drug user – what was he trying to erase? In court, he said he drank because he wanted to forget. Forget what? And why so many versions of the killing? The question that must have haunted jurors was what Colgan had really done. It must have been something substantial to be charged with first-degree murder.

But once the defence got past Colgan, they'd have to deal with the almost irrefutable evidence of Andrea Wiwcharuk, a consistent witness who held up extremely well under cross-examination. All the defence could do was hope to show her to be a liar, something most people probably wouldn't believe. Or they could have let Johnston admit he made those statements but say he was imitating what Houghton, Colgan or Manger told him at an earlier time.

Colgan and Immunity

Probably the question that needs answering most is why the Crown picked Colgan to deal with – a man who had sexually assaulted, unlawfully confined and kidnapped the girl. He was a chronic alcoholic, a drug-trafficker, and the weakest man of the four. The answer, evidently, was that he was the only one who would talk, and would do so only if he were sufficiently intimidated, as he was when slapped with a charge of first-degree murder.

"They [police] knew in the end they had to get one of these people to confess," Johnston's lawyer Greg Brodsky said. "It's the luck of the draw. There's no reason to really pick Colgan. They could have picked Johnston to testify against Colgan or Johnston to testify against Houghton – they could have picked anybody to finger anybody else."

It raised the question: could the Crown have made a deal with the wrong man? Did police wait sixteen years to convict the man who may have helped in the beating of Osborne but wasn't the one who did the actual stabbing? But Colgan's lawyer, Don MacIver, defended the deal of immunity. "You don't deal with the man who wielded the screwdriver," he said.

To this day, granting Colgan immunity is a sore point with police and the Crown, who won't admit it was a power play. As George Dangerfield puts it, "There was none of that crap going on around here." Chief investigating officer Bob Urbanoski insists he charged Colgan with first-degree murder because he believed him to be the killer, not as part of a power play by the Crown and police. "The Attorney General's department wouldn't authorize the charges if that was the case," he said.

If that truly is the case, what's wrong with our police force? The deal was the Crown's strategy. The deal they wanted was that Colgan would accept being charged as an accessory after the fact. "It's absolutely ridiculous to think the Crown would believe a man would take partial immunity," former Attorney General Roland Penner said.

Perhaps the saddest point of all is our perverse justice system, one that allows a man like Colgan to help make it work. If it weren't for Colgan, police would never likely have gotten a conviction against Johnston or anyone else for that matter and the case would have remained unsolved. Colgan, in his own bizarre way, helped turn the wheels of justice by taking the deal and testifying.

Houghton

What is very suspicious is Colgan's help for Jim Houghton – the man he was supposed to turn evidence against. Throughout the trial, Colgan protected his friend, almost to the point of clearing him. Word had it that Colgan wrote a letter to Scurfield exonerating Houghton, but it was never used in court.

There's no reason why the letter would be used. The Crown's own key witness exonerated Houghton. That was their evidence. In short, it appeared that Colgan not only made a deal with the Crown; he might have also made some type of arrangement with Houghton's lawyer, John Scurfield. It is possible that Colgan felt so badly about turning evidence against his longtime friend that he turned around and tried to help him out.

Colgan insisted throughout the trial that Houghton was a nice guy and was just trying to help the girl. And for all Colgan knew, Osborne was dead by the time Houghton got out of the car. It was a ridiculously unbelievable argument, but one the jury bought, probably because Houghton looked like a big teddy bear and Scurfield was so convincing. "I could see he [Colgan] was trying to protect Houghton – it was inevitable that he should be nice and sincere to him," Brodsky said.

Scurfield, who has a tendency to go as far as he can and just a little bit further, often went overboard and was told by Justice Schwartz several times during the trial to stop blaming Johnston for the killing. From his point of view, his strategy of blaming Johnston was clever and got his client off. But is that how our justice system works? Do you get your client off at all costs and not give a damn about anything else?

If Colgan made two arrangements – one with the Crown

and another with Houghton – it's something that would actually help the prosecution's case. The Crown would be almost guaranteed a conviction against Johnston if Colgan and Houghton agreed to back up each other's stories. Did the Crown want two convictions or the guarantee of getting at least one, Johnston? Was the Crown double-dealing?

Inconsistencies

There were a number of things that just didn't make sense in the trial. The first one was how Johnston would know where a screwdriver was in someone else's car.

Colgan, to this day, has no idea where police got the blood-drenched screwdriver found near the scene and the second one found days later – both screwdrivers presented in court. "He swears it [the screwdriver used to kill Osborne] was thrown in the bush," said MacIver.

Dr. Donald Penner, the pathologist, said in court that it was unlikely the screwdriver identified as the murder weapon by Colgan caused the 5.5 centimetre gash into Osborne's skull and brain. It was more likely that the second screwdriver presented in court could have done that damage. How many screwdrivers were used and was the one in court the real murder weapon?

Then there's the question as to why Johnston would want to sexually assault a Native girl when he had been, for the most part, indifferent to them. Johnston didn't really hang around with the other three socially, so why would he suddenly become the ringleader of intimidation? Or were the other men beating up Osborne and Johnston decided just to clean up the job?

Did Johnston's size 8 1/2 foot make any of the 11 1/2, 12, and 12 1/2-inch impressions in the snow? If Houghton was such a sweet guy, what was he doing driving Osborne to his parents' cabin and later to the site of Betty's death? Where did the blood in the back seat come from? How is it that Manger can't remember anything about the killing and Colgan has it down so pat sixteen years later? Why does Colgan insist he didn't know Betty Osborne when her boyfriend, Cornelius Bighetty, remembers them all being together on several occasions?

It is difficult, if not impossible, to believe that Colgan, Houghton, and Manger were listening to the radio and drinking a bottle of wine while Johnston was beating and stabbing the girl. Clearly, more than one man was involved in the killing. Whether Bielert had two sets of footprints written in his notes produced in court is not all that important — Knight had remembered a set of footprints on either side of the drag marks. Two men dragged Betty Osborne to her death and one of them is walking free. "Two people were involved — we're speculating which two," Brodsky said later.

The most horrifying aspect to this murder is that three other men were there — three men who drove away from a badly wounded woman and left her for dead. None faced charges of unlawful confinement, kidnapping, accessory after the fact, or sexual assault — they all walked away from murder without punishment. At least one of them, however, helped drag Betty Osborne to her death and likely helped beat and stab her. One very dangerous man is out there, walking the streets, and merrily living his life. Three men all helped rob Betty Osborne of life, yet they are entitled to live theirs comfortably and fully, without retribution, without even having to spend a single moment's thought on it.

Police Investigation

One thing the public can't understand, and quite justifiably, is why it took sixteen years to solve a case when just about everybody in town knew who had been involved.

Roland Penner, the former attorney general, said it's because the police didn't pursue the murder vigorously.

"Had they acted more expediently and speedily, they wouldn't have had to make a deal [of immunity]," Penner said.

The reason for the apparent apathy, Penner says, is because Betty Osborne was Native. Had the girl been white and her killers Native, there would have been tremendous outrage from townsfolk in The Pas. "I'm sure it [murder investigation] would have been much more vigorous if she was white," Penner said. "Native people have every right to feel the way they do."

And, Penner says, townsfolk likely wouldn't have kept the deadly murder confessions to themselves if the murdered woman had been white. He declares that out and out racism allowed Betty Osborne's killers to walk.

"People still ask me," said one resident, "Come on, did everyone in town really know who the killers were?' and I said, 'Yeah, we all knew but we didn't say anything.' "

But assistant commissioner Dale Henry refutes Penner's comments. He insists there was no racism involved in the police investigation and that the RCMP pursued the case relentlessly. "If the officers were Native and the girl was white it wouldn't have been investigated any differently," he said.

Native leaders, the public, and the former attorney general have blamed police for not pursuing the case vigorously enough because the woman was Native. While this is just conjecture, constables on the case appeared to be overzealous if anything, physically abusing and harassing suspects and constantly reminding the men of their involvement in the killing. It was every cop's dream to break this murder – it was a glory case – and their ticket out of The Pas rural detachment.

While the police techniques were dated at best, it is up to a constable's superior to instruct subordinates on new techniques or assign them to the case full-time. Most of these cops were very young, with just five years under their belts – they needed strong direction and manpower to work on the case full-time. Understandably, it's tough for a cop to investigate a murder of this stature along with his regular workload of suspicious drownings, armed robberies, attempted murders, and dozens of other crimes.

Someone should have been giving the policemen constant direction and putting a few of them on the case full-time until it was solved. If anyone is to blame for the delay in solving the crime, it's the constables' superiors, who have the power to make things happen. This was proved years later when they put Bob Urbanoski, a relentless and determined constable, on the case. Waiting sixteen years also cost the Crown one valuable witness, Phillip McGillivary, who died of old age before he could testify.

Had there been stronger direction from the top, it probably wouldn't have taken seven months to get a search warrant for the Colgan car. Police insisted they didn't have enough to get a search warrant until mid-June. That's difficult to believe, considering they had four digits of a six-digit licence plate and a witness who saw the vehicle leave the murder scene. As well they had three suspects, Colgan, Houghton, and Manger, in mind. At one point in the investigation there were six prime suspects. Johnston didn't become a suspect until later. At the very least, it's bizarre.

Police sent screwdriver drinks to suspects, mailed some of them screwdrivers at Christmas and religiously pestered the four in an attempt to evince murder confessions. While this shows police at least worked on the case, their methods were ridiculously out of date and obviously not working. Ripping open an anonymous Christmas present to find a green-handled screwdriver wasn't about to prompt Colgan to dial 911.

But it's up to a constable's boss to tell him to do otherwise and teach new techniques – especially cops this young and inexperienced. It is the corporals and sargeants who tell cops when they have enough to get a search warrant, Crown attorneys who tell them when it can go to a preliminary hearing, and the assistant police commissioner who puts a cop on the case full-time.

No one did that until 1983, when Bob Urbanoski took over the file, determined to solve the case. And he did, sixteen years after the fact, without a shred more evidence than had been available in 1972.

"It took someone like Urbanoski to take the bull by the horns," lawyer Don MacIver said.

Urbanoski deserves full marks for getting the case to court and pursuing it relentlessly. But it should have been done years earlier with instructions, more help from the higher-ups and the same limitless budget.

From 1971 to 1983, the higher ranks of the RCMP obviously hadn't thought it necessary to put someone on the case full-time, instead giving it to cops to look at in their spare time.

This case was a great embarrassment to the RCMP and they finally jumped on the murder at a time when emotions among the Native community were running high. What a coincidence! Was this good politics rather than an attempt at justice? If it was, it didn't work. Natives and the public were outraged to discover three men had walked.

The public can't even be satisfied that the man who drove the screwdriver through Betty Osborne fifty times is the one in jail. There were too many inconsistencies in testimony to be sure Johnston was the only killer.

During Johnston's appeal on September 9, 1988, Mr. Justice Joseph O'Sullivan of the Manitoba Court of Appeal said he had no doubt Johnston was the murderer. "The evidence is overwhelming, in my opinion, that your client killed the woman," he told lawyer Greg Brodsky. Even if Johnston were to have a new trial, O'Sullivan speculated that, "The jury would at least have returned a verdict of manslaughter. There's no question that if the man killed this girl, he should be punished."

While the three appeal court justices – O'Sullivan, Chief Justice Alfred Monnin and Mr. Justice Sterling

Lyon – listened to Brodsky's argument in favour of a new trial, they also speculated about why the jury hadn't found Houghton guilty.

"Four men took a woman to the country and she died there," O'Sullivan said. "It raises an inference all four are guilty of murder."

Brodsky argued that Johnston should get a new trial because one day after his conviction, the Supreme Court of Canada struck down Section 213(d) of the Criminal Code, which allowed for a conviction of murder in any case where death resulted during the commission of a serious offence such as sexual assault or robbery. Brodsky said the trial judge, Mr. Justice Sidney Schwartz, had told jurors they could find Johnston guilty of murder even if he killed Osborne accidentally during a sexual assault.

The court's response was quick and unanimous. Five days later the decision, written by O'Sullivan, was delivered, discussing, dismissing Brodsky's request for a new trial:

In my opinion there was no error in the instructions which the trial judge gave to the jury. The other points raised by the appellant are, in my opinion, without merit. The appellant complained of the address made by counsel for another accused who was acquitted. In my opinion, there was no error on the part of the trial judge in dealing with this point.

There is no doubt on the evidence, in my opinion, that the accused killed the victim and the nature of the assault shows that the accused killed in a frenzy, meaning to inflict bodily harm which he knew would result in her death. It is possible, I think, that the accused's mind was befuddled by alcohol and drugs to the extent that he did not mean to cause death but the defence of drunkenness was adequately put before the jury and there is no reason to disturb its verdict.

In this case, four young men joined in abducting a

young women and at the very least they stood by while one or more of them killed in a wanton and brutal assault.

O'Sullivan added that, ''A third man, Houghton, who, in my opinion, surely was at least guilty of confining the accused, was acquitted by the same jury that found the appellant [Johnston] guilty.''

Obviously disturbed that only one of four men had been convicted, he concluded by questioning the laws that allowed them to escape unpunished despite the roles they'd played. He even suggested that others who knew about the crime but said nothing should be accountable for their actions. In his closing statement he wrote, ''It seems to be that this is a clear case which shows that Canadian law is deficient in that it is no longer an offence to conceal a felony. In my opinion, lawmakers should consider whether it is not time to reinstate the offence of misprision of felony. That would render illegal the conspiracy of silence which covered up the murder for sixteen years on the advice of a lawyer.''

O'Sullivan's recommendation would make it a criminal offence for a person to hear a confession of murder and not report it to police. According to Winnipeg lawyer Heather Leonoff, it is ''an extraordinarily outdated concept.'' Leonoff said the last time it was used was in 1955 when the courts tried to charge a man with a felony because he refused to tell police who had assaulted him. The charge didn't hold up because the court said Parliament had abolished felonies. It's a law that could cause some difficulties, said Winnipeg lawyer Jack London. For one, lawyers would likely have to be excluded from it, otherwise they couldn't properly serve their clients because they couldn't guarantee them confidentiality. As well, it would be almost impossible to enforce, he said. ''The Federal Law Commission feels they [the public] should be required to disclose information,'' London said.

"But it would be impossible to enforce. It would be unfair and too ambiguous to define a law that way."

Despite its outdated concept or possible complications, it is a law that could have seen Osborne's killers brought to justice and prompted the sheriff formally to report the murder confession nine years earlier. Even if it is a law that would be impossible to enforce, it is one that could prompt members of the public to go to police with val-. uable information for fear of prosecution.

Meanwhile, the dismissed appeal has prompted Patricia Johnston to question her husband's innocence and she is still grappling with what she will do with her life. Some of her relatives understandably believe Johnston is the killer and have told Patricia, "You're lucky it wasn't you." Patricia is having second thoughts about waiting for her husband's release. In a bizarre turn of events, however, Johnston's former girlfriend, Arlee White, has pledged her love and promised to wait for him if his wife chooses not to. Arlee, who believes in Johnston's innocence, is regularly visiting him at the penitentiary, hoping he will want to build a life with her once he has been freed. In the meantime, Brodsky has recommended his client ask for leave to appeal to the Supreme Court of Canada.

The Pas residents refuse to admit there was ever a conspiracy of silence, saying instead that only a select few knew who was involved in the killing. Mayor Bruce Unfried said he is worried the town has been tarnished by the scandal. "There are people who feel wrongly implicated," Unfried said. He wants a public inquiry into the murder to explain the deal of immunity, and why it took so long to bring the case to trial. While Unfried hopes such an inquiry might help save the town's reputation, The Pas deputy mayor Wes Maksymetz says that although he's sickened that townspeople had information and didn't go to police, he doesn't want a public inquiry. "I can't see what it would solve other than raking the town through the coals again,'' he said (His cousin, Steve Maksymetz, admitted to hearing a confession from Colgan.)

Natives see Osborne's murder quite simply: they say four men were involved and four men should be in jail. It's difficult for them to rationalize how three walked away from murder. It's especially confusing for Betty's thirty-four-year-old brother, Isaiah Osborne, who named his first daughter Helen Betty Osborne. ''I'm doing time for something that's not as bad as murder and three others got off,'' he said in an interview in the penitentiary. ''It's not fair that those guys can walk away from killing my sister.'' Even though he's had similar run-ins with the law before, he doesn't understand why he's serving thirty months in a maximum-security penitentiary for two counts of robbery and assault causing bodily harm. (He punched two people at a party in Norway House and stole thirty-three dollars from one of them.)

To this day, the family still grieves Betty's death. Cecilia often cries about the murder, saying she has been robbed of a sister she dearly loved. She has few memories of Betty, she says, except for the funeral and Betty's favorite song, ''Me and You and a Dog Named Boo.'' Other things have changed in the Osborne household: Justine gave birth to another daughter, Joan, by Jimmy Osborne. Her husband Joe, whom she left more than eighteen years ago, has had a stroke. Justine visits him in a rest home.

If it weren't for lawyer D'Arcy Bancroft, the four men may not have made a pact of silence. ''D'Arcy gave those young men the best legal advice they could get,'' former partner Bob Mayer said. ''If they would have followed his advice, nothing would have happened.''

Natives can't understand, however, why Bancroft represented all four men, threatened police, and did his best to see that the murder investigation ground to a halt. As well, they can't understand how a legal system could allow every Native to be rejected from the jury panel at the trial once it finally took place.

It is this case and an overall feeling of injustice among Natives that prompted former NDP Attorney General Vic Schroeder to launch a two-man justice inquiry into the treatment of Indians under Manitoba's criminal justice system. Native leaders initially wanted a full public inquiry but were somewhat pacified after the announcement of the two-man commission, largely because it included a Native judge.

Formally called the Public Inquiry into the Administration of Justice and Aboriginal People, the two commissioners, Mr. Justice Alvin Hamilton of the Court of Queen's Bench and Provincial Court Associate Chief Judge Murray Sinclair are supposed to place special emphasis on the Betty Osborne case and the fatal police shooting of Native leader John Joseph Harper in Winnipeg on March 9, 1988. The timing of this inquiry was remarkable, coming in the middle of an election campaign and considering the fact that the NDP were failing miserably in the polls.

The $1.5-million commission, which is to submit its report to the government by October 1989, has the power to call witnesses in determining whether police, courts and jails discriminate against Natives. It plans to visit various Manitoba communities to hear from the people directly.

It is to review policing of Native people, including arrest and charging procedures, their access to legal counsel especially in remote communities, court processes such as bail and custody and plea bargaining, and court dispositions such as comparing dispositions among Natives and non-Natives.

It will also look at post-sentencing, including the comparative success of Native versus non-Native groups on probation, the use of halfway houses, reintegration into communities and reserves, Native awareness and knowledge of the justice system, and employment of aboriginal people in the system.

However, it has already been fraught with difficulties. The Assembly of Manitoba Chiefs, which represents Manitoba's sixty-one bands, had asked the government for $140,000, in addition to $100,000 they received from the federal government, to hire a legal adviser and to pay for travel, research, and other expenses. Without the extra funding the assembly said that the Native leaders couldn't prepare themselves to make presentations at the inquiry, which was expected to travel to fifty communities. Progressive Conservative Attorney General Jim McCrae said he saw no need to duplicate work the commission would be doing and refused to give them the funding.

Schroeder said the aboriginal inquiry could result in the altering of some provincial laws, if deemed necessary by the two-man commission. In any event, Premier Gary Filmon and his Progressive Conservative government will have to deal with its recommendations. During the first few months of the inquiry, Native people have alleged that they have been given gag orders not to testify. Some have made presentations, although they fear repercussions from their superiors in the Attorney General's department. Native leaders such as Oscar Lathlin, chief at The Pas Indian Reserve, are dismayed. "It's not going the way I expected it to," Lathlin said. "With the news of the sheriff getting his job back, I think we're all getting fed up. Things aren't going to change."

Shortly before the announcement of the commission, the RCMP conducted its own internal investigation, as did the NDP Attorney General's department. Both have refused to release it until they receive word as to whether the Supreme Court of Canada will hear Johnston's second appeal.

But many of the details of the RCMP report were leaked out after Deputy Attorney General Tanner Elton and a few other cabinet ministers went to The Pas in February 1988 to meet with The Pas town council and

The Pas Indian Band in an apparent attempt to soothe their feelings. Needless to say, they didn't. In short, the RCMP report, not surprisingly, said the Mounties had pursued the case vigorously for sixteen years and had handled it properly.

Whether the two-man commission will shed any new light on the justice system or the investigation of Betty Osborne's murder and her killers' subsequent trial is doubtful.

Justice failed Betty Osborne; four white boys and a silent town conspired against her. A foreign world stole her dignity little by little, until finally, it killed her. Then it tried to ignore her murder.

MAIN CHARACTERS

Helen Betty Osborne: The victim, a nineteen-year-old Cree high school student from Norway House.

The Men

Lee Colgan: An admitted alcoholic, failed drug trafficker, and thief. A father of two children.

Jim Houghton: A pot-bellied frontiersman, industrial salesman, and married father of two children. What friends called a nice guy.

Dwayne Johnston: A long-haired, bearded biker, rebel, and a tough guy who hates "rats." A married father of two children.

Norm Manger: A vagrant drunk who sleeps in laundromats and under porches when all else fails.

Their women

Linda Hardy: The middle-aged brunette who fell in love with Norm Manger.

Shannon Houghton: The vivacious brunette, totally devoted to her husband Jim Houghton and oblivious to his carryings-on.

Pat Johnston: The pretty wife of Dwayne Johnston and mother of his two children.

Arlene Karlenzig: The ex-wife of Lee Colgan and mother

of his two children, who dumped him after receiving one beating too many.

The Town and the Reserve

D'Arcy Bancroft: The four-hundred-pound brilliant, eccentric lawyer, who instructed Colgan, Houghton, Johnston, and Manger to make a pact of silence about Osborne's murder.
Patricia Benson: Betty Osborne's landlady in The Pas.
Cornelius Bighetty: Betty Osborne's lover.
Harold "Bud" Colgan: Lee Colgan's father, a meek and mild man, manager of the liquor control commission store in The Pas.
Joyce Colgan: Lee Colgan's overbearing mother, who would do anything for her son.
Art Fishman: Lee Colgan's boss.
Cecilia Osborne: Betty Osborne's sister.
Isaiah Osborne: Betty Osborne's brother.
Joe Osborne: Betty Osborne's father.
Justine Osborne: Betty Osborne's mother.
Andrea Wiwcharuk: A woman who waited fifteen years to tell police she'd heard what sounded like a murder confession from one of the men at a party.

The Investigators

About two hundred RCMP officers who also worked on the case off and on for sixteen years, including:
Corporal Harold Bielert: The identification officer.
Constable Thomas Boyle: The officer responsible for the corpse.
Sergeant John Fitzmaurice: The officer who obtained the search warrant for the death car.
Sergeant Larry Grosenick: The supervisor of the murder case sixteen years ago.

Constable Donald Ray Knight: The chief investigating officer of the Osborne murder in 1971.
Corporal Vance Menhennit: Handler of Buck, the tracker dog.
Constable Bob Urbanoski: The cop who broke the case wide open sixteen years later.
Dr. Donald Penner: The pathologist who said Osborne's murder must have been the work of a frenzied killer.

The Judiciary

Mr. Justice Sterling Lyon: The Appeal Court judge who presided over Johnston's appeal.
Judge William R. Martin: The provincial court judge who authorized a search warrant for the death car.
Chief Justice Alfred Monnin: Chief judge of the Manitoba Court of Appeal who presided over Johnston's appeal.
Mr. Justice Joseph O'Sullivan: The Appeal Court judge who presided over Johnston's appeal.
Mr. Justice Sidney Schwartz: The judge of the Court of Queen's Bench of Manitoba who presided over Johnston's and Houghton's trial.
Judge Kris Stefanson: The provincial court judge who presided over Johnston's and Houghton's' preliminary hearing.

The Prosecution

George Dangerfield: Senior Crown Attorney.
Daniel Dutchin: Assistant Crown Attorney.

The Defence

Greg Brodsky: Counsel for Dwayne Johnston.
Donald MacIver: Counsel for Lee Colgan.
John Scurfield: Counsel for Jim Houghton.

ACKNOWLEDGEMENTS

In my research I have received generous co-operation from Pat Johnston and her husband, Dwayne Johnston, the man convicted of murdering Helen Betty Osborne. Thanks to Arlene Demmings for providing valuable insight into her ex-husband Lee Colgan, the man originally charged with first-degree murder for the crime; to Shannon Houghton, wife of Jim Houghton who was tried for the killing and acquitted; and to Linda Hardy, common-law wife of Norm Manger, the fourth man involved in the killing of Osborne.

I would like to give special thanks to Greg Brodsky, lawyer for Dwayne Johnston, who was extremely generous and of invaluable assistance to me throughout my research. Thanks to my lawyer David Wolinsky for his excellent advice and moral support; to Donald MacIver for his insights (like Mr. Brodsky, he has given me every assistance consistent with the requirements of duty to his client); and to Provincial Court Judge William Martin.

Thanks also go to the Winnipeg *Sun*, whose help came through when I needed it most; to RCMP assistant commissioner Dale Henry and his staff, including Bob Urbanoski, Thomas Boyle and former RCMP officer Donald Knight.

Thanks to Dr. Donald Penner, who kindly reviewed some medical matters; to Roland Penner, former Attorney General; to the chief medical examiner Peter Markesteyn and his staff; to Bob Mayer for his insights on former law partner D'Arcy Bancroft. Thanks to Cornelius Bighetty and his brother Pascall for their reminiscences and to Isaiah and Cecilia Osborne for sharing memories of their sister, Betty. Thanks to Art Fishman, Harold Dent, Gord Goodings, Hersh Wolch, Brian Roque, Diane Alstad, Joe Guy Wood, Heather Bird, Don Obe, and Brad Powell. I have also received assistance from a number of others who would prefer that I not thank them by name.

Heather Robertson's book *Reservations Are For Indians* was of tremendous assistance to me in my research. It brought to life the Norway House that Betty Osborne grew up in during the late 1960s, and The Pas she later moved to. Thanks to Charis Wahl of McClelland & Stewart whose editing and advice were a great help to me.

Finally, I would like to thank Stephen Ostick for his thoughtful editing and for being a confidant and best friend to me throughout this project.

Unavoidably, mistakes in emphasis and interpretation may have crept in, but in all instances I have done my best to mirror what went on in The Pas during and after the murder of Helen Betty Osborne.